Music in America

∞

EXPERIENCING MUSIC, EXPRESSING CULTURE

∞

ADELAIDA REYES

New York   Oxford
Oxford University Press
2005

Oxford University Press

Oxford   New York
Auckland   Bangkok   Buenos Aires   Cape Town   Chennai
Dar es Salaam   Delhi   Hong Kong   Istanbul   Karachi   Kolkata
Kuala Lumpur   Madrid   Melbourne   Mexico City   Mumbai
Nairobi   São Paulo   Shanghai   Taipei   Tokyo   Toronto

Published by Oxford University Press, Inc.
198 Madison Avenue, New York, New York, 10016
www.oup.com

Oxford is a registered trademark of Oxford University Press

Library of Congress Cataloging-in-Publication Data
Reyes, Adelaida
      Music in America: experiencing music, expressing culture/Adelaida Reyes.
      p. cm.—(Global music series)
      Includes bibliographical references and indexes.
      ISBN 0-19-514666-2—ISBN 0-19-514667-0 (pbk.)
      1. Music—United States—History and criticism. 2. United States—Social life
and customs. I. Title. II. Series.

ML200.R48 2004
780'.973–dc22   2004050099

Printing number: 9 8 7 6 5 4 3 2 1

Printed in the United States of America
on acid-free paper

GLOBAL MUSIC SERIES

General Editors: Bonnie C. Wade and Patricia Shehan Campbell

Music in East Africa, Gregory Barz
Music in Central Java, Benjamin Brinner
Teaching Music Globally, Patricia Shehan Campbell
Carnival Music in Trinidad, Shannon Dudley
Music in Bali, Lisa Gold
Music in Ireland, Dorothea E. Hast and Stanley Scott
Music in the Middle East, Scott Marcus
Music in Brazil, John Patrick Murphy
Music in America, Adelaida Reyes
Music in Bulgaria, Timothy Rice
Music in North India, George E. Ruckert
Mariachi Music in America, Daniel Sheehy
Music in West Africa, Ruth M. Stone
Music in South India, T. Viswanathan and Matthew Harp Allen
Music in Japan, Bonnie C. Wade
Thinking Musically, Bonnie C. Wade
Music in China, J. Lawrence Witzleben

Contents

Foreword

In the past three decades interest in music around the world has surged, as evidenced in the proliferation of courses at the college level, the burgeoning "world music" market in the recording business, and the extent to which musical performance is evoked as a lure in the international tourist industry. This heightened interest has encouraged an explosion in ethnomusicological research and publication, including the production of reference works and textbooks. The original model for the "world music" course—if this is Tuesday, this must be Japan—has grown old, as has the format of textbooks for it, either a series of articles in single multiauthored volumes that subscribe to the idea of "a survey" and have created a canon of cultures for study, or single-authored studies purporting to cover world musics or ethnomusicology. The time has come for a change.

This Global Music Series offers a new paradigm. Teachers can now design their own courses; choosing from a set of case study volumes, they can decide which and how many musics they will cover. The series also does something else; rather than uniformly taking a large region and giving superficial examples from several different countries within it, in some case studies authors have focused on a specific culture or a few countries within a larger region. Its length and approach permits each volume greater depth than the usual survey. Themes significant in each volume guide the choice of music that is discussed. The contemporary musical situation is the point of departure in all the volumes, with historical information and traditions covered as they elucidate the present. In addition, a set of unifying topics such as gender, globalization, and authenticity occur throughout the series. These are addressed in the framing volume, *Thinking Musically*, which sets the stage for the case studies by introducing ways to think about how people make music meaningful and useful in their lives and presenting basic musical concepts as they are practiced in musical systems around the world. A second framing volume, *Teaching Music Globally*, guides teachers in the use of *Thinking Musically* and the case studies.

The series subtitle, "Experiencing Music, Expressing Culture," also puts in the forefront the people who make music or in some other way experience it and also through it express shared culture. This resonance with global history studies, with their focus on processes and themes that permit cross-study, occasions the title of this Global Music Series.

Bonnie C. Wade
Patricia Shehan Campbell
General Editors

Preface

"America" is both a geographic location and a concept, both a tangible, measurable place and an idea subject to interpretation. In either sense the term inevitably affects what one can call American music. This book follows the common usage that takes the United States and its people to be the "America" referred to by those who would have God bless it as well as by those who protest its presence and influence overseas. It is a usage illumined in part by the contrastive designation "the Americas" when reference is being made to North, Central, and South America.

There is, however, a more specific usage that this book favors. "America" is used here to underscore the distinction between the nation and the state. The importance of the distinction particularly in the case of the United States requires a more extended discussion, which is found in chapter 1. It is mentioned here only to introduce a fact often forgotten or ignored but one that has a potentially critical impact on what "American," when applied to music, includes. The boundaries that define the nation as the cultural realm in which music resides (the sense in which "America" is used here), do not necessarily coincide with those that define the state (the United States). The boundaries of the nation, responsive to aesthetic and moral standards, tend to be fluid. The boundaries of the state as territory and its jurisdiction as a government responsive to legal standards are kept relatively fixed. For the purposes of this book, therefore, and in the spirit indicated above, America is a people who "*believe* they are related" (Conner 1993: 1, emphasis added) and whose country of residence is the United States.

America's musical culture is relatively young, and its musical life is lived in a vast land, in a country that likes to call itself a nation of immigrants. Much of its self-definition, musical and otherwise, draws not from a single mythical or demonstrable cultural lineage but from an ever growing number of such lineages. People from many different cultures who "speak" different musical languages embark on the process of becoming American in their musical life even as they continue to use sounds and musical systems that were born and are still in use elsewhere. Removed from social and historical context and treated as sound alone, these sounds often belie their new functions and meanings the way ethnic foods or non-Caucasian faces obscure an underlying American core. They make up a complex fabric that finds simple expression in the question, What does America's music sound like? The challenges one faces to explore that question are many, because America's music is a perennial work in progress, ceaselessly and restlessly emergent. Those who choose to explore the subject must therefore envision the whole, based on past and present realities.

Like all the authors in the Global Music Series, I have sought salient themes to weave multiple threads together in the effort to answer that question. The country's motto, *E pluribus unum* (Out of many, one) is powerfully suggestive: diversity, unity, and identity. *Identity* is the core issue of the question, What does American music sound like? *Diversity* is what makes that question necessary: America as a nation of immigrants and a lover of innovation keeps adding new ingredients to its mix. The sounds of multiple cultural origins trying to find their place in a national culture raises questions of identity that are peculiarly American. *Unum* is what makes the term "America" and its derivative "American" come to existence and remain in existence to designate a nation and a culture. I deal with each of these themes separately in the book, although all three—in tandem or in conflict—run throughout the work in one form or another.

I have written this book with two major purposes. I have sought a perspective from which to take in the whole picture, but I have not followed the path of other textbooks on American music. I do not trace a chronological sweep of history, nor do I systematically discuss musical repertoire and genres. One aim has been to explore where America's music comes from, who makes it, for what purpose, and for whom, for these are what shape sound and make it music. All musical culture is a matter of space and time, of geography and history, and of the people who use music to express themselves within a community that considers that music theirs. It is a matter of sound given meaning through use in social and historical contexts. I also aim to nurture a way of seeing and hearing that is informed by the sweep of American history. This, along with its outstanding dynamism, shapes and reshapes American musical life.

The choice of musical examples on the CD are, unfortunately, constrained by the affordability of obtaining permissions from commercial record companies. But increasingly, this handicap is being overcome by the availability of legal downloads on the Internet. A growing number of students are becoming adept at downloading, using their own computers, computers in school, or those in libraries. Suggested examples will therefore be part of the text, with CD titles and catalog numbers given whenever possible to facilitate either acquiring, borrowing from the library, or downloading. It is also hoped that the flexibility of the book's approach, which allows teachers to make substitutions and students to bring in complementary materials, will help make up for the absence of some musical examples from the CD.

ACKNOWLEDGMENTS

Heartfelt thanks to Bonnie Wade for giving me the challenge to grapple with the infinite complexity of a subject that promises to stimulate and educate me long after this book is completed, and for seeing me through the process; Patricia Shehan Campbell for her encouragement; Kai Fikentscher for having gone through the manuscript with a fine-tooth comb and for providing me with parts of a work in progress to use as an example of a remix; Tomie Hahn for having so generously provided me with pictures of "Pikapika" and information on the DVD of the work; Jason Kao Hwang whose help was crucial in obtaining permission for the use of his work; Kay Kaufman Shelemay, Doris Friedensohn, and the manuscript reviewers for their invaluable feedback; and the many people who, in their generosity, have given me permission to use their materials for illustration. They will be named as their materials are used in the text.

CD Track List

1. "God Bless America" by Irving Berlin. Arranged and conducted by Nelson Riddle, sung by Kate Smith. From *The Best of Kate Smith* (Curb Records D@-7745), track 1. (P) Originally recorded Prior to 1972, All Rights Reserved by BMG Entertainment. Courtesy of the RCA Records Label, Under License from BMG Special Products. © Copyright 1938, 1939 by Irving Berlin. © Copyright renewed 1965, 1966 by Irving Berlin.

2. "Yankee Doodle" (traditional), Sung by Pete Seeger. From *American Favorite Ballads*, vol. 1 (Smithsonian Folkways SFW 40150).

3. New Women's Shuffle Dance (*Askaanyea guynawsay*), by Young Nation (Seneca) Gary Parker, leader. From the recording *Creation's Journey. Native American Music* Smithsonian Folkways 40410, provided courtesy of Smithsonian Folkways Recordings. (c) 1994. Used by Permission.

4. "Oye como va" by Tito Puente. Tito Puente and his orchestra. Field recording, Summer 1981 (New York City) by Adelaida Reyes.

5. "Pretty Polly" (traditional). Sung with guitar by E. C. Ball. Recorded by Alan and Elizabeth Lomax in Rugby, Virginia. From *A Treasury of Library of Congress Field Recordings* (Rounder Records), track 3.

6. "One Morning in May" (traditional). Sung by Texas Gladden. Recorded by Alan and Elizabeth Lomax in Salem, Virginia. From *A Treasury of Library of Congress Field Recordings* (Rounder Records CD 1500), track 17.

7. "Diamond Joe" (traditional). Sung by Charlie Butler. Recorded by John A. Lomax in Parchman, Mississippi. From *A Treasury of*

Library of Congress Field Recordings (Rounder Records CD1500), track 24.

8. "Soldier's Joy" (traditional). Performed by the Nashville Washboard Band. Recorded by Alan Lomax in Nashville, Tennessee. From *A Treasury of Library of Congress Field Recordings* (Rounder Records CD 1500).

9. "Oh, Susanna" by Stephen Foster. Sung by Pete Seeger. From *American Favorite Ballads*, vol. 1 (Smithsonian Folkways SFW 40150).

10. "Go dating with my love" (anon.) for Chinese bamboo flute. Performer not known. From *Chinese Bamboo Flute Music* (Legacy International CD 366), track 5.

11. "Bittersweet Music" by Bun-ching Lam, performed by Paul Taub on piccolo. From *Mountain Clear Water Remote. Music of Bun-Ching Lam* (Composers Recordings, Inc. CD 726), track 2.

12. "Batey" by Tania Leon in collaboration with Michel Camilo. Performed by The Western Wind Vocal Ensemble, Puntilla, and New Generation with Daniel Ponce (conga), Eri Charlston, and Joseph Passarro (percussion), conducted by Tania Leon. From *Blessings and Batey* (WW 2001 © The Western Wind Vocal Ensemble).

13. "Hello Song" by Yup'ik (Eskimo) made and sung by Nicholas R. Charles, Sr. From the recording entitled *Creation's Journey: Native American Music*, Smithsonian Folkways 40410, provided courtesy of Smithsonian Folkways Recordings. © 1994. Used by Permission.

14. "Aloha e ke kai o Kalalau" (traditional). Sung by Emily Kau'I-o Makaweli-ona-lani-o-ka-Mano-o-kalani-po-Kukahiwa Zuttermeister, Noenoelani Zuttermeister Lewis, and Hau-Olionalani Lewis. From the recording entitled *Hawaiian Drum Dance Chants*, Smithsonian Folkways 40015, provided courtesy of Smithsonian Folkways Recordings. (c) 1999. Used by Permission.

15. "U. S. Highball" by Harry Partch. Thomas Coleman (Mac) and Gate 5 Ensemble conducted by Jack McKenzie. From *The Harry Partch Collection*, vol. 2 (Composers Recording, Inc., CD 752) track 1.

16. "The Letter" by Harry Partch. Performed by Harry Partch, voice and ensemble. From *The Harry Partch Collection*, vol. 2 (Composers Recording, Inc. CD 752), track 3.

17. "Banshee" by Henry Cowell. Performed by Henry Cowell. From *Henry Cowell: Piano Music* (Smithsonian Folkways SF 40801), track 9.

18. "The Gong on the Hook and Ladder" by Charles Ives. Eva Gruesser and Mia Wu, violins; Rachel Evans, viola; Beverly Lauridsen, cello; Joel Sachs, piano and bass drum. From *Charles Ives the Visionary* (Musical Heritage Society/Continuum MHS 512292Y), track 4.

19. "Goodnight, Irene" by Huddie Ledbetter (a.k.a. Leadbelly). From *Folkways: The Original Vision* (Smithsonian Folkways SF 40001), track 15.

20. "This Land Is Your Land" by Woody Guthrie. Sung by Woody Guthrie. From the recording entitled *This Land Is Your Land: The Asch Recordings*, vol. 1, Smithsonian/Folkways 40100, provided courtesy of Smithsonian Folkways Recordings. (c) 1997. Used by Permission.

21. "I ain't got no home" by Woody Guthrie. Sung by Woody Guthrie. From *Folkways: The OriginalVision* (Smithsonian/Folkways SF40001), track 4.

22. "Gray Goose" (traditional). Sung by Leadbelly. From: *Folkways: The Original Vision* (Smithsonian/Folkways SF 40001), track 14.

23. *Cuban Overture* by George Gershwin. The New York Philharmonic Orchestra, conducted by Zubin Mehta. From *Gershwin* (Warner/Erato 8573-84518-2), track 12.

24. Clave pattern. Field recording, summer 1981 (New York City), by A. Reyes.

25. "We Shall Overcome" by C. A. Tindley. Sung in a 1964 mass meeting, Hattiesburg, Mississippi. From disc 1 of the recording entitled *Black American Freedom Songs, 1960—1966* (Smithsonian Folkways 40084), provided courtesy of Smithsonian Folkways Recordings. © 1989. Used by Permission.

26. "Swanee River" by Stephen Foster. Sung by Pete Seeger. From *American Favorite Ballads* (World of Music 12504 AAD), track 4.

27. "Stars and Stripes" by John Philip Sousa. New England Music Camp Symphonic Band, Leon Gregorian, conductor. Courtesy of New England Music Camp Administration.

28. "Maple Leaf Rag" by Scott Joplin. Kate A. Katigbak, piano. Courtesy of Kate A. Katigbak.

29. "A Lincoln Portrait" by Aaron Copland. James Earl Jones, speaker; Seattle Symphony and Chorale, conducted by Gerard Schwarz. From: *Portraits of Freedom: Music of Aaron Copland and Roy Harris*. (Delos International DE 3140), track 2.

30. "Barbara Allen" (traditional). Sung by Pete Seeger. From *Pete Seeger: American Favorite Ballads*, vol. 2 (Smithsonian Folkways SFW CD 40151), track 1.

31. "Caverns" by Jason Kao Hwang and the Far East Side Band. From *The Far East Side Band Caverns* (New World Records 80458-2), track 1. (P) 1994 Recorded Anthology of American Music, Inc.

32. "Stomp Dance" by Carlos Nakai and AmoChip Dabney. Carlos Nakai, flute; AmoChip Dabney, saxophone. From *Edge of the Century* (Canyon Records CR-7034), track 9. Courtesy of Canyon Records, 3131 West Clarendon Ave., Phoenix, AZ 855017 (www.canyonrecords.com). Published by Native American Flute Music (ASCAP) and Left Minded Music (BMI).

33. (a) An excerpt from "Mart" by Ali N. Askin. (b) "Mart(-inique)," a remix by Kai Fikentscher, with technical assistance from Ron Vannoy. Courtesy of Kai Fikentscher.

CHAPTER 1

A Unifying Vision

Have you ever wondered if "God Bless America" (CD track 1) is an American song? Probably not; its title and lyrics virtually give its "nationality" away. What about "Yankee Doodle" (CD track 2)? Or the Iroquois "New Women's Shuffle Dance" song (CD track 3)? Listen to a sampling of Tito Puente's "Oye Como Va" (CD track 4).

Are these pieces of music American? How can one tell?

People who have pondered the question of American musical identity have used a number of features as clues. Some of these clues are not musical, such as the language of the song lyrics or the nationality or ethnicity or place of residence of the composer. Some clues are musical. There are, for example, folk and traditional tunes and national anthems, or characteristic rhythms such as those of ragtime, or an entire form such as jazz and the blues. How far do such clues go toward establishing American musical identity?

"God Bless America," which came close to achieving the status of a national anthem around the time of World War II, was written by Irving Berlin, who was born Israel Baline in Russia—no one seems to know exactly where, probably western Siberia. His family, which was Jewish, came to this country when Berlin was a child. He grew up to become one of the most successful songwriters in the history of American musical theater. He has more than one thousand compositions to his credit, among them "Alexander's Ragtime Band," "This Is the Army, Mister Jones," and *Mr. President*.

No one seems to know either the composer or the precise origin of "Yankee Doodle." It was called a "national air" in a 1782 collection by James Aird, *Selection of Scotch, English, Irish and Foreign Airs, for the Fife, Violin, or German Flute*, which was published in Glasgow. No composer has been noted there, and it has been passed around, as folk songs are, ever since.

The composer of the "New Women's Shuffle Dance" song is also unknown, though he or she is almost certainly Native American. In most cases, individual authorship is less important to Native American musical identity than is the communal function of the music. The song heard on CD track 3 is usually sung when the shuffle dance, which reflects the high regard in which women are held by the Iroquois Haudenosaunee, is performed.

"Oye como va," a song with Spanish lyrics, became the signature piece of Tito Puente, who was born of Puerto Rican parents and grew up in New York City's East Harlem. He was a formally trained musician and studied at the famous Juilliard School of Music in New York City. He went on to make his name in Latin American music, jazz, and the hybrid style called Latin jazz.

ACTIVITY 1.1

There are numerous examples of pieces that can make one wonder if the piece is American. Listen to El Salón México, *an orchestral work by Aaron Copland. A famous composer who was born and studied in New York City, his strongest influence came from Paris, where he also studied with the famous French teacher Nadia Boulanger. For* El Salón México *he made use of Mexican folk music materials. Listen, too, to "Con Alma," another Spanish-title piece. It is by Dizzy Gillespie, the South Carolina–born virtuoso trumpet payer who influenced such other jazz greats as Miles Davis and Thelonius Monk. Gillespie also left his mark on what came to be known as modern jazz.*

Bring in other examples, specifying what makes the musical identity of each ambiguous (language of text, birthplace, musical features, etc.). What makes each example possibly American? What other musical identity do the clues suggest?

Much more can be said about each of these musical examples. But what they indicate collectively, as a body, better introduces the challenges one faces in inquiring about America's music. Features that would ordinarily serve as clues to identity give conflicting signals instead. The unreliability of national origin as such a clue is exemplified by "Yankee Doodle," commonly believed to be American. What if it were in fact born in Ireland or Scotland or some other land? Would it suddenly become un-American? In the case of "Oye como va," the language of the text and the ethnicity of the composer point to a Latin identity, while Puente's place of birth, his education and his lifelong residence in the United States suggest an American identity. Only "God Bless America," by its text, and the shuffle dance song, by its musical style, give clear indications of cultural identity, yet their musical styles are radically different.

In this small sample, then, one glimpses as through a peephole the vast arena that is American music, and a fundamental problem presents itself: How can the diversity of national and ethnic origins, and their cultural content as expressed in a multiplicity of musical languages, share a common identity? How can the seemingly endless variety of musics in American musical life become one as the country's motto, *E pluribus unum*—out of many, one—suggests they are or should be? Even a sample of musical items as tiny as that with which this chapter begins becomes a reminder that Americanness in music is a far greater and more fascinating challenge than meets the eye or the ear.

The challenge grows in magnitude as more and more people from different cultures, bringing different musical sounds and systems, become Americans, and as Americans themselves create ever changing grounds for identity construction. Who is an American?, a question long debated, has never been fully resolved (Foner 1998: xx). The question of authorship or ownership comes up: Who makes America's music and, through the circumstances of its use, affirms its Americanness? These questions reverberate throughout the voyage of discovery that the study of America's music always turns out to be. But one thing has already become evident: sound alone does not suffice as a distinctive marker of American music. How then is it to be recognized?

ACTIVITY 1.2

Imagine yourself a member of a distant culture introduced to the American scene for the first time. For a week, listen to and take note of the music you hear—in supermarkets, concert halls, churches, synagogues, temples, streets; on the radio, on TV, or anywhere else you happen to be. Compile as exhaustive a list as as you can of the music and musical events announced in newspapers, posters, and flyers distributed in public places and pinned to bulletin boards. Visit a record store and browse through the bins and shelves. (Keep your list for future use.)

At the end of the week, write a letter to a friend who is not an American describing what you have come to regard as "American music."

THREE THEMES

Three themes have emerged from the brief exploratory paragraphs above that could serve as a point of entry into an exploration of America's musical life: *diversity, identity,* and *unity* or *oneness.* In subsequent chapters, I will discuss in detail their role in shaping the character of America's music. For now, it suffices to allude to their importance.

Not only is diversity highly observable in the American scene, but it is also evident from even the few musical examples discussed above. In the country's motto, *E pluribus unum,* diversity is announced as a principle on which the nation is built. Where diversity prevails, and where being different is a mark of both the individuality that the nation cherishes and the multiculturalism that the country promotes, a commensurate need for identity arises. The persistence of the question, Who is an American?, and its correlate, What is American?, attests to this. Unity or oneness is an expression of identity on the national level. It is both historical reality and aspiration. It was embedded in the Union, the name by which the country was known long before it came to see itself as a nation called the United States. At the same time, it represents the nation's image of itself projected into the future. Diversity, identity, and oneness, singly and together, are therefore the guiding themes of this book and important markers for those who would navigate the complexities of American musical life.

A VOYAGE OF DISCOVERY

All voyages call for a destination or an objective, and for the voyage on which this book is about to embark, the eminent historian George M. Frederickson has made a case for one. Although his concern was with American history, his idea speaks to America's musical culture as well. What is needed, he writes (2002: 37), is a unifying vision—unifying because America's parts are so diverse and mutate so rapidly; a vision because the sum of those changing parts cannot but be transitory and ultimately illusory. In its musical as in its social life, America's impatience with the here-and-now keeps it reaching out for innovation, revising the present, and moving toward a future that can only be indeterminate. It is for good reason that America has often been described as a perennial work in progress. I have decided to strive for a unifying vision in this book by putting at the forefront ideas and principles that have proven to have historical validity for America. Pieces of music and events drawn from actual musical life will illustrate them. I have adopted this approach in the service of a unifying vision. Taking this approach is also my acknowledgment that a book this size cannot begin to accommodate a full account of even the most significant parts that make up the whole of America's music.

The Perspective.   It is often said that the way a thing looks depends on one's perspective—on where one stands, physically and psychologically, as one looks. In pictures of the Earth taken from outer space in the second half of the twentieth century, for example, the most glorious man-made structures and national symbols fade into insignificance, as the eye is drawn by the panoramic sweep of the planet as a whole. But from a lesser distance, say, from a passenger plane, a substantial portion of the view recedes, and things that had hardly been visible now gain in size and stature and may even dominate the scene. At ground level, what from outer space was hardly a speck can now become the whole picture. Perspective draws the frame around what the whole picture is to be.

The musical *Sunday in the Park with George* by Stephen Sondheim (b. 1930) illustrates these points as they apply to music. Premiered in 1984 on Broadway, the work was acclaimed as ground-breaking in the world of musical theatre. It has come to be considered a classic.

Long regarded as homegrown and American (despite some influences from Europe's operetta), the musical comedy was initially considered a popular genre that combined speech and song. It was considered lightweight, serving more as entertainment than as a call for thoughtful, aesthetic engagement. It was out of place in an opera house. Now evolved into musical theater, it combines features of serious or "legitimate" theater with the musical complexity of opera, at home on the Broadway stage as in opera houses. Sondheim has gained recognition as the foremost composer of musical theater today.

Sunday in the Park with George revolves around a fictionalized version of Georges Seurat (1859–91), the neoimpressionist French painter

FIGURE 1.1 *Georges Seurat, French, 1859–1891.* A Sunday on La Grand Jatte. *Oil on canvas, 207.6 × 308 cm.* *(Helen Birch Barltlett Memorial Collection, 1926, 224.* The Art Institute of Chicago. *All rights reserved.)*

who pioneered a painting technique called pointillism and was considered one of the most innovative artists of his time. His most famous work is *A Sunday Afternoon on the Isle of La Grande Jatte* (figure 1.1). The musical's principal character, named George, is, like Seurat, an advocate of pointillism, which calls for dabbing innumerable dots onto the canvas. (In the musical, George complains of the numbness of his wrist caused by that repetitive action.) In a humorous reference to George's preoccupation with dots, the musical's heroine is named Dot.

Two scientific principles backed Seurat's use of pointillism. One was the finding by the American physicist O. N. Rood that "color mixed by the eye is more intense than pre-mixed color" (Holt 1966: 468). The other comes from the science of optics: *at a certain distance* from the painting, the *viewer's eye* will make the dots appear to come together. The painter thus relies on the viewer's eye to blend tiny islands of pure color so that they form subtly colored, shaded, and seemingly solid images and landscapes.

When the painter set out to create the picture, he had a unifying vision: the images on the canvas arranged and colored in a particular way.

This unified whole is what the painter meant the viewer to see, and it becomes visible at the right distance, from the right perspective. Should the viewer change his or her perspective by moving too close, the picture "disappears," replaced in the viewer's eye by the dots. The single whole that is the picture becomes instead a collection of dots, each a whole in itself.

ACTIVITY 1.3
Watch the first act of Stephen Sondheim's Sunday in the Park with George *(VHS Image Entertainment, no. 4585 MB). Listen carefully to the words of "Color and Light" and to what George strives for in a work of art (CD: RCA 5042). Watch him as he dabs bits of color to his canvas. It is a demonstration of pointillism's technique. The aural equivalent comes when George sings the song that begins "Red red red red," which is discussed below.*

Like a pointillist painting, American musical life, figuratively speaking, consists of dots. (Recall the experience of listening to the music around us.) Up close, each piece of music, each repertory, or each genre is, like pointillism's island of color, an island of sound. Removed from the perspective at which the eye (in music's case, the ear, and ultimately the mind) can connect the dots and fuse their colors, the islands of sound appear unrelated. The artists chosen in 2001 as National Heritage fellows illustrates this (figure 1.2). One is a Creole zydeco button accordionist; another is a Beijing opera performer; still another is a Japanese *taiko* drummer; and yet another is a Kiowa singer. How are they and the other yearly honorees, and the musical traditions they represent, all parts of an American national heritage? The National Endowment for the Arts, a U.S. government agency, has recognized them as such.

ACTIVITY 1.4.
Locate the National Endowment for the Arts (NEA) on the Internet. Find the process and criteria for selecting National Heritage Fellows, to understand how the NEA has articulated a na-

FIGURE 1.2 *National Heritage Fellows, 2001. Among them are Wilson "Boozoo" Chavis, Creole zydeco accordionist (top row, frame 3); Qi Shu Fang, Beijing opera performer (top row, frame 4); Peter Kyvelos, oud (Middle Eastern lute) maker (row 2, frame 1); Eddie Pennington, thumb-picking-style guitarist (row 2, frame 4); Hazel Dickens, Appalachian singer-songwriter (row 3, frame 1); Joao Grande, capoeira master (row 4, frame 1); Seiichi Tanaka, taiko drummer (row 4, frame 2); Fred Tsoodle, Kiowa sacred song leader (row 4, frame 4).*

tional cultural policy. Also, find out what artists have been selected in other years.

The question cries out for a unifying vision: What connects pieces or bodies of music? What unifies the growing diversity of American musical life? Sondheim and Seurat suggest that the questions involve not only "what" but "who" as well, for there comes a point when everything on a canvas or a score or in any given medium falls short of the *experience* of art, visual or aural. *Someone* has to be there listening, seeing, creating, judging, perpetuating, nurturing, or killing through sanction or neglect. Someone is needed to make individual musical dots "move" from their disconnectedness as islands to connectedness as parts that come together to create the American musical scene. Seurat's viewer, Sondheim's listener—people, not just their products but their capacity to respond—matter greatly. Musical culture cannot exist without them, just as a painting cannot exist without painters and viewers.

Sondheim's *Sunday in the Park with George* has more to say.

At one point, George sings staccato, the choppiness and grammatical disconnectedness of which is the aural representation of quick dabs of color (note also the fragmentary, repetitive, instrumental equivalent):

> *Blue blue blue blue*
> *Blue blue blue blue*
> *Even even*
>
> . . .
>
> *Bumbum bum bumbumbum*
> *Bumbum bum*
> *More red*
> *More blue*
>
> . . .
>
> *Red red red red*
> *Red red orange*
> *Red red orange*
> *Orange pick up blue*
>
> . . .
>
> *Dut dut dut*
> *Dot Dot sitting*
> *Dot Dot waiting*
> *Dot Dot getting fat fat fat*
> *More yellow*
> *Dot Dot waiting to go*
> *Out out out. . . .*

It is especially tempting to see each word as an insular world because each seems to stand outside the rules of grammar and syntax; the words do not connect to make up sentences. But as in the case of the dots in a pointillist painting, there are principles of organization at work that transcend the wholeness of a single word or a single dot. The picture's frame defines the arena within which the painter can deploy the images into a visual composition. The principles that govern pointillism—the viewer-object relationship and the laws of optics—allow the painter-viewer collaboration to create a new and larger whole, in essence a new meaning, over and above those represented by the dots and the pure color that they hold.

By extension, the Sondheim examples permit us to look at the American musical scene as framed by the American nation-state. It is full of individual pieces or groups of pieces, moving restlessly within the frame. But until principles of order are brought to bear, no large picture will emerge.

This is the point at which context becomes essential. Owing to the multiplicity of musical languages in use and the social forces to which music and musicians respond when they deploy their materials, the search for the order that underlies a unifying vision reaches out beyond sound into other sources of clarification. The who and the what of America's music must find their roles and their meaning within the larger story of the nation.

The Historical Context. The historian Eric Foner once famously remarked that when people become interested in national identity, they turn to history. The core of Americanness—that centripetal force that keeps together the endlessly splintering, metamorphosing parts of the American musical scene even as those parts are flung afield by the centrifugal force of individual creativity responding to the irresistible lure of new ideas—is embedded in the history of the American nation-state. That history is, among other things, a history of expectations—expectations powerful enough to condition what observers look for and what stands in the way of discovery.

It would have been reasonable to expect that the country that was to become known as the United States would be modeled along the lines of the European nation-state. It was, after all, the dominant model in the eighteenth-century world into which the United States was born. That model assigned a high value to cultural homogeneity, which, it was believed, would ensure that the laws of the state would be understood and hence more easily obeyed by all. The nation, built on beliefs, language, and norms of behavior shared by people who believe themselves heirs to a common heritage, and the state, seat of government and sovereign territory, can thus be regarded as one.

The power of this model was such that the oneness of nation and state was codified in formulas such as "one nation, one state." The term *nation* came to stand for both. The name of world bodies like the League of Nations and the United Nations bears testimony to the persistence of this belief, which has left its mark on music scholarship. Musics have been labeled as though they were single, culturally indivisible units (e.g., Chinese music, Indian music, etc.). Outside influences have been thought of as foreign bodies, threats to the purity of a music's "bloodline." Music, like the nation-state and its language, have been presumed governed by a single system that suffices to account for all of musical life.

But the circumstances leading to the creation of the United States make the fit between that life and European expectations far less than perfect. More than anything else, what the early colonials who rebelled against the British to become Americans shared was not a belief in but a profound distrust of centralized authority. John Higham, one of the leading historians of America and American culture, memorably observed that unlike European nation-states, notably Germany, the American union was not built on a sense of peoplehood. In fact, it took more than a decade after 1776 before a national government could be created and almost a century to get the states under one American umbrella (Higham 2001). Lacking a preexisting set of shared beliefs and traditions, the new nation's cultural bonds had to be constructed around a political creed, an ideology.

Creating a sense of peoplehood was rendered extremely difficult and, hence, further delayed by demography and geography. The high degree of decentralization and a small, highly mobile population pushing the frontiers of a territory that was expanding north, south, and west combined to minimize the opportunities for human interaction that conventional community and nation building requires.

History has thus underscored the distinction between the American nation and the American state. Assumptions of cultural homogeneity are nowhere as relentlessly debunked as they are in the United States. "This is America," its citizens like to say as they flaunt not only the country's difference from all others but Americans' difference from each other as well. The flippant remark has strong historical roots. Underscoring the contrast between the United States and European nations, "where the primacy of the nation over the individual imposed general uniformity," the Harvard professor of social science Liah Greenfeld points to "the unchallenged primacy of the individual [in the United States, which] guaranteed plurality of tastes . . . and self-definitions within the national framework. Pluralism was built into the system" (1992: 482).

Diversity thus replaces cultural homogeneity at the center of the American scene. Pluralism is the national birthright. It is a principle that American society upholds no matter how flawed its implementation. Out of diversity arises a need to define and redefine identity both on the level of the individual and on the level of the nation where oneness and its stability as principle are continually challenged by changing forms and actors on the national scene. Diversity, identity, and oneness are themes that cut across American history and American life, and any account of America's music must take them into consideration. They hold the key to a unifying vision, to coherence in a life that on some levels seems to move at warp speed, even as on other levels it moves at history's majestic pace.

CHAPTER 2

Diversity and American Musical Life

In the American musical scene, diversity has an in-your-face quality. More than any other attribute of American musical life, it stands out. It is relentless in its demand for attention, and indeed it is impossible to ignore. Musical products of all kinds proliferate, and competition is acted out in its most unforgiving forms as all kinds of music fight to be heard in their struggle for survival or social approval. In the realm of popular music, the jostling is for a place in the charts, for bestsellerdom and its promise of fame or notoriety and possibly wealth. Newness, a partner of planned obsolescence, reigns. In the realm of art music, a quieter though no less intense jostling is for respect and recognition among one's peers, a place—lasting, if possible—in concert programs and history books. In the realm of folk or ethnic musics, the jostling is more for the loyalty and affection of a constituency than for material gain. Or perhaps each of these kinds of music wants a piece of what every other overtly reaches for. "Lend me your ears" is a message that the American market trumpets in an endless variety of forms to announce a new musical product—a recording, a performer, a sound, even a revival.

How can one address this complex musical landscape? One possibility is to try to account for its content. A list or an inventory of traits, genres, activities, compositions, or personages can yield only that—outsize and growing, to be sure, but a list nonetheless and needing constant updating to boot. Like names in a phone book, a list is indifferent to relations between items and hence a poor mirror of what makes the items add up to a dynamic, coherent musical life.

What diversity is made of is constantly changing. Perhaps, then, the more pertinent inquiry for a brief work such as this is to inquire into *how* in the American context diversity becomes cultural wealth rather than a tower of Babel, a chorus of voices performing in mutually incomprehensible tongues. Thus I will direct attention less to the genres and people who inhabit the musical scene and more to the roles, func-

FIGURE 2.1 *Glimpses of America's diversity: (a) a Vietnamese concert in the yearly summer festival in Lowell, Massachusetts; (b) a Spanish guitarist; (c) an American percussionist in a New York subway station.* (Photo by A. Reyes)

FIGURE 2.1 *Continued*

tions, and processes, to the circumstances and forces, social and historical, that motivate people to express themselves musically in varying
contexts. These motivating factors are what make the story recognizable no matter what the inevitable changes that come into its retellings,
no matter the changes in the way the actors shape the look and the
sound of the musical scene. But all this must be placed in a setting, a
time and place that makes what all actors do easier to understand.

DIVERSITY AND AMERICAN IDEOLOGY

One of the most brilliant connoisseurs of American life, Alexis de Tocqueville (1805–59), called egalitarianism—the precept that all men are

created equal—the defining principle of American life. With the enthronement of that principle—an ideal or a myth that will always fall short of full realization—Americans opened the door not to uniformity but to diversity. By breaking the social bonds of rank, profession, and birth, American egalitarianism offered freedom from those limits imposed on what one can make of oneself. This was fertile soil for individualism (a term attributed to Tocqueville) and its creative powers. It gave rise to a spirit suffused with the restlessness of those released from the constraints of patronage-dominated societies such as nation-states have customarily been. Frontier living—literally and metaphorically—flourished in the climate of the new country's egalitarian ethos and produced a population devoted to innovation and free enterprise.

From individuals, to groups, to government, the conditions that favored diversity spread throughout the land. James Madison, one of the Founding Fathers, was explicit about the need for factions. In one of the Federalist Papers, Madison advocated a diversity of interests to guard against the dominance of any one group that can then have the power to trample on the rights of the rest. This homegrown, internally generated diversity manifested itself most commonly in regional types: the New England Yankee, the southerner, the westerner, the midwesterner, the rural and urban folk among others, all keenly aware of how they differed from one another. Values and especially religion were strong grounds for differentiation. Southern Protestant whites set themselves apart from Catholics, Jews, and immigrants; slave owners and abolitionists apart from each other; whites and blacks likewise. Like James Madison, Justice Oliver Wendell Holmes, one of America's most eminent jurists, saw diversity not just as a natural consequence of people with different cultures, countries of origin, and beliefs sharing common territory. He saw it as essential to America's democracy.

SOURCES OF DIVERSITY

In recent decades, the most written- and talked-about source of diversity is external: through immigration. True to the country's egalitarian ideals, Americans consider citizenship as an equalizer: ideally, everyone, regardless of national origin, shares the same status as an American. Immigration ebbs and flows however, as a result of forces from within the country as well as from external circumstances. Laws are altered from time to time, permitting, restricting, or blocking the influx of people from abroad. Prejudice and differing interpretations of ideology condition the way immigrants are received, the way people relate to one another. As late as the mid-1950s the country was still wondering, "Whom Should We Welcome?," the name of a study commissioned by President Dwight Eisenhower. The question continues to resonate.

The sources of diversity, one internally generated and the other originating from outside the country, are thus interlinked. Together they create a synergy—a combination that makes the whole greater than what the great African American writer Ralph Ellison called the sum of its diversities. The result is the extraordinary cultural diversity that observers see as a defining feature of America's musical life.

ACTIVITY 2.1
Listen again to CD tracks 1–5. Revisit the musical items you collected for the activity in chapter 1. You may add more items if you wish. Create two lists: one of musical items that you think represent internally generated, homegrown diversity, the other of musical items that you think represent diversity that comes from the infusion of imported elements. Do not be concerned if you find items that straddle the two lists and that do not clearly belong to one or the other. The reasons will become clearer as the chapter proceeds and you look more closely into American musical diversity. But be prepared to defend your placement of items squarely on one list or the other.

You have just embarked on a rudimentary kind of classification—a sorting-out that is prerequisite to finding order. At least one other activity will build on what you have just done, so hold on to the results of this exercise.

It is nonetheless useful to look at the two major sources of diversity separately. For like all synergies, much depends on what each brings to the equation. The people who animate those sources, having different points of departure, develop different conceptions of the social and musical world to which they belong, the place they hope to occupy, and the road map they need to use in order to get to where they want to be.

Immigration.   Until the early nineteenth century there were no legal restrictions to entry into the country, and the bulk of immigrants were from northern Europe: Scots, Irish, French, Dutch, Germans, Scandinavians, and also Spaniards came to settle in the new nation. After the Civil War (1861–65), immigrants came as well from southern and eastern Europe: Italy, Greece, Austro-Hungary, Russia, and the Balkans. The only sizable group that was not European was the Chinese who began trickling into the States shortly after Independence to work in the gold fields. They arrived in considerable numbers to work in the railroads beginning in the second half of the nineteenth century.

For the better part of the nation's first hundred years, then, the range of diversity was culturally broad but politically and racially narrow. Philip Gleason notes, for example, that in the early days of nation building, when Africans and Native Americans were excluded from the national community, the great majority of the population was white (mostly of British stock) and Protestant (1980: 56). While we have been accustomed to identifying those groups by nation-state of origin, many of the immigrants identified themselves at a more local level as Calabrians, Sicilians, and Neapolitans rather than as Italians, or as Saxons, Westphalians, and Württemburgers rather than as Germans. Scots-Irish, the source of much early recorded American songs, were Scots who had settled first in Ireland before migrating to America.

CD tracks 5, 6, 7, and 8 exemplify the early sounds of diversity. Collected by John Lomax, his son, Alan, and Alan's wife, Elizabeth, with the support of the U.S. Library of Congress, the items, now considered traditional American songs, are the closest approximations we have of how they must have sounded before the days of recording technology. The British provenance of CD tracks 5 and 6, however, is confirmed by British scholar-collectors who found that many folk songs that had disappeared in England were conserved in the American South, in Appalachia, and in other isolated communities.

"Pretty Polly" (CD track 5) is a British broadside, that is, a ballad printed on a large sheet called a broadside. "One Morning in May" (CD track 6) is an Anglo-Irish broadside, sung in traditional ballad-singing style: unaccompanied, dispassionate. "Diamond Joe" (CD track 7) is a field holler, unaccompanied, intended for solitary work in the field and almost by definition a rural form. It is associated with early African Americans who, although not considered part of the American community, had access to and became accessible to white music making, the result of serving in white households or living and working in white-owned plantations. "Soldier's Joy" (CD track 8) is an ensemble piece with voice and a band consisting of objects used in daily living—a wash-board (percussion), a lard can (bass), a tin-can fiddle—as well as a banjo-mandolin and guitar (Wade 1997). Originally a pragmatic impulse that took what was available and assigned it a musical function, the wash-board in particular subsequently was incorporated into urban music making.

ACTIVITY 2.2
Compare CD tracks 5–7. Pay particular attention to the time organization, the vocal quality, the dynamic range, the shape or contour of the melodic line (curvilinear or angular), the way the pitches are articulated (whether they are approached directly or whether the singer slides toward the pitch), the form, and the text-tune relationship. Rank them according to similarities and differences. Would you consider them similar enough to be directly related the way members of a nuclear family are? Or would you consider their differences to be significant enough to justify placing them in different "families"? Support your response by citing musical and other (e.g., historical) features.

Following the Civil War, immigration steadily gained in importance as a factor that shaped and determined the content of American musical diversity. The magnetic pull of the ideals of equality and pluralism was complemented at certain times by needs from within the United States—the need for labor, for example. At other times, social factors such as the fear of growing heterogeneity on the part of early twenti-eth-century Anglo-Americans (Barton 2001: 84) blocked the entry of po-tential immigrants. Changing internal conditions and attitudes deter-mined how widely or how narrowly the country's doors would be open to immigration. But the growing presence and increasing visibility of minorities eventually forced into the open the tension between the in-clusivity of the ideal and the reality of exclusionary practice. This ten-sion has run through American history to the present day.

Forced Migration.   Migration is now a generic term that covers move-ments of people within a nation-state (internal migration) and between nation-states (immigration). On that general level, and especially in cases of immigration, distinctions between people who migrate of their own volition and those who are forced to leave by circumstances beyond their control are not evident. But the reasons for which people move can be significant in the way they react to their new environment—in the way they shelter or share their culture, the social relations they forge, and the various ways they adapt to the American scene.

The image of America evoked by symbols such as the Statue of Liberty is that of a nation of voluntary migrants who responded to the lure of this "land of opportunity." But a large number of migrants left their home country and were brought to the States against their will. The African slaves best exemplify America's forced migrant population both in their numbers and in their continuing impact on American life and vice versa.

Originally regarded as property and not as "constituent members of our society," as Edmund Randolph, the country's first attorney general, put it (Foner 1998: 39), their entry into American society seemed foreclosed. But the Civil War and the issue of slavery exposed both the degree to which black and white America were polarized and the terrible schism that separated American ideology from reality. The 1790 census painted the country black and white, acknowledging only one migrant/racial category among five: white males sixteen years and older; white males less than sixteen years; white females; other white persons; and slaves. Not until 1860 were two distinct racial categories added to which Chinese and American Indians could belong.

The social stigma attached to blackness blinded American society to the wealth of cultural resources that Africans, in the diversity of their cultural origins, brought with them. For decades after their arrival, their impact on American cultural life was minimized to almost total insignificance by strict rules of segregation and the pervasive devaluation of what the African cultures had to offer.

Although not as violent as the Civil War, the 1960s civil rights movement echoed that war as representation of a racially segregated America. That movement reminded the country at large that race cut such a deep fissure in American society that multiple cracks had built up around it, segmenting the social and political landscape. But racial conflict, the starkest icon of America's contradictions, also ignited the kind of conflagration that encourages new growth when the fires finally die down. Social relations between black and white America, marked both by harmony and conflict, has bred a variety of musical types and genres. Field hollers (e.g., CD track 7) are believed to be a precursor of the blues. Ragtime, spirituals, and gospel music; black-inspired works by white musicians such as minstrel songs (CD track 9); and musicals or operas like Scott Joplin's *Treemonisha* and George Gerswin's *Porgy and Bess* became part of the American musical scene. But perhaps even more remarkable was the emergence of what the rest of the world has identified as a commingling of black and white America and an unarguably American form: jazz.

Stephen Foster (1820–64), born in Pittsburgh of Anglo-Irish descent, a devotee of Western European composers such as Mozart and Beethoven but largely self-taught, became one of the most prolific songwriters of his time. He was best known as a writer of so-called household songs—songs meant to be enjoyed at home—and of minstrel songs, of which "Oh Susanna" far outlived its composer.

ACTIVITY 2.3

Analyze "Oh, Susanna" (CD track 9) as you did CD tracks 5, 6, and 7. Place it in the "family" where, on the basis of its musical features, you think it most likely belongs.

While race relations have therefore generated some of the most disruptive forces in the country's history, those relations have also produced important and extremely powerful instances of cohesive tension. For this reason, the thread of African American life that entered the fabric of American culture with the forcible migration of Africans to the States will be picked up again in chapter 4, when the spotlight moves from the "pluribus" of the country's motto toward the "unum."

Voluntary Migration. The nation-of-immigrants concept of America conjures the image of a nation that is invariably welcoming to all immigrants. This idealized picture homogenizes the experience of migrants and hides the varying degrees of acceptance or hostility that greeted the migrants upon their arrival. Often used as model in narratives of the immigrant experience in America, that picture fails to give due consideration to the ways in which different attitudes on the part of the host population evoke different responses on the part of the newcomers, resulting in different rates and forms of immigrant adaptation to American society. Two contrasting groups—the Irish and the

Chinese—provide a fleeting view of the experience of initially not-too-welcome voluntary migrants. Both began coming to the States early in the country's history. But each had to contend with a different reception from the American host society. Their experience exemplifies how local conditions and attitudes can inhibit or facilitate migrant contributions to the country's diversity.

The influx of a substantial number of Irish, most if not all of whom were Roman Catholic, at the beginning of the nineteenth century provoked the resident Anglo-American Protestant majority into acts of discrimination that frequently took violent forms. Catholic churches were burned; Irish were called Negroes turned inside out (Patterson 2000: 15). The intensity of the social friction took a long time to subside. But the Irish stayed on, and slowly, with race, language, and relative familiarity with the ways of the dominant culture on their side, the Irish made their way to the American mainstream (see the Hast and Scott *Music in Ireland* volume in this series). More intense and prolonged than the hostility shown the Irish was that shown the Chinese, the first sizable group of Asians who came to America. Coming to the States to try their luck when gold was discovered in the West, the Chinese were subsequently augmented by new arrivals who came to work as laborers. The Chinese were separated from the larger American society by a wide racial and cultural chasm that proved unbridgeable in the nineteenth century. The Chinese were not allowed to own property, and citizenship was not an option. Anti-Chinese riots underlined the intolerance, and by 1882, with the enactment of the Chinese Exclusion Act, which barred the entry of Chinese into the United States, the negative sentiments were translated to law. The ban was in effect for the next sixty-one years.

Not surprisingly, Chinese music during that period, confined as their makers and users were to Chinatown enclaves, was hardly more than an exotic artifact to Americans until well into the next century. Chinese music was *in* America, then, but not *of* it until political and ideological changes intervened.

This anonymous tune recorded in California in 1993 and heard in CD track 10 was adapted from a Chinese folk song and played on a Chinese bamboo flute (*dizi*; also transliterated as *di tse* or *di tze*). While a song would have afforded better comparability with the previous examples, one of the most obvious differences between those and a Chinese song—the language of the text—needs no illustration. A more practical reason for this choice is comparability with the following Chinese example.

FIGURE 2.2   *Ricky Yeung Wai-Kit playing the* dizi.   *(Used with permission of Ricky Yeung Wai-Kit.)*

ACTIVITY 2.4

A generalization that is often made about Chinese melody is that it is pentatonic. Try to count the number of different pitches you hear in CD track 10 in order to say whether that is true in this case. Check the recording for these features as well: the dynamic range, the quality of the attack on pitches (whether they are consistently or mainly "hit on the head," as was the case with "Yankee Doodle" in CD track 2, or the performer slides to and from pitches), and the shape of the melodic line (whether smooth or angular). Compare it to the examples cited earlier in this chapter and consider to which group you have designated as a "family" it may belong.

Changes in the political climate in the twentieth century induced changes in immigration laws; that, in turn, had a strong impact on who gets to play in America's musical arena. During the Cold War, refugees and immigrants from communist countries were given preferential treatment for entry into the United States. For humanitarian reasons and in recognition of the propaganda value of people "voting with their feet" to reject their country's government, the United States opened its doors to people from communist regimes. The Chinese Exclusion Act of 1882 thus faded into history. Quotas on admission into the country, which came into effect in 1921 and which excluded Asians in general (as opposed to the earlier specifically Chinese-directed Exclusion Act) while favoring those from northern and western Europe, gave way to immigration reforms in 1964–65. Chinese musicians, among others, were given access to American institutional support. Beijing opera found audiences not only in Chinatowns and areas with large Chinese populations but also in the concert halls and public venues of American society at large. (Note the inclusion of a Beijing opera star in the roster of National Heritage Fellows of 2001; see figure 1.2). For the first time, the freedom to interact at all levels of American musical life—a freedom that immigrants from Western Europe had enjoyed from the start—could now be enjoyed by Chinese immigrants as well. Bun-ching Lam's career and "Bittersweet Music" exemplifies the result of such interaction (CD track 11).

Born in 1954 in Macau, a Portuguese colony now reverted to China, Bun-ching Lam was trained in music at the Chinese University in Hong Kong. She moved to the United States in 1976 and received a Ph.D. in composition from the University of California in San Diego. A pianist herself, she writes for Western instruments while also collaborating with Chinese musicians and performers.

"Bittersweet Music" combines the capabilities of the Western piccolo with the sounds and sensibilities of the Chinese *dizi*. In this piece, the customary pitch inventory of the piccolo, which consists of the pitches of the Western musical scale, is altered to recall the customary "language" of the *dizi*, which "bends" the pitches of the Western scale and uses intervals smaller than the standard Western semitone.

ACTIVITY 2.5

Analyze or describe "Bittersweet Music" using the musical features with which you analyzed CD track 10. Compare the two pieces. Would you say they belong to the same "family"? Give your reasons.

Do a mini-field project and try to find Chinese vocal music from a local source—live or recorded. Find out as much as you can about the musicians and the music for a report to the class.

The inroads made by Chinese music into American musical life are reflected in a 2001 lead article in *The New York Times* Arts and Leisure section entitled "The Sound of New Music Is Often a Chinese Creation" (April 1). It was probably inspired by the two Academy Award nominations and the Oscar for the original score for the film *Crouching Tiger, Hidden Dragon* (2000), won by the Chinese composer Tan Dun. But what the article made clear was that American receptivity to the music Chinese musicians make is not a fluke. Besides Tan Dun there are others, such as Bright Sheng, who teaches composition at the University of Michigan at Ann Arbor and whose opera on Madam Mao Zedong was premiered in 2003 at the Santa Fe opera. The works of Bun-ching Lam have been performed at Lincoln Center and elsewhere. Fred Ho is gaining recognition in the jazz music field. Chinese composers are winning commissions for large works—operas, symphonic works, concertos— from prestigious institutions such as the Santa Fe Opera, Spoleto USA, the Metropolitan Opera, and the New York Philharmonic. There have been at least three Chinese musicians recognized as National Heritage Fellows since the awards were initiated in 1982.

Because it had a longer and more arduous road to travel to gain admission into American musical life, Chinese music provides an important opportunity to assess the necessity of invoking extramusical factors as tools to understanding America's musical diversity in general. Legislation affecting immigration goes a long way to explain why American diversity sounds as it does. By acting as gatekeeper, immigration policy determines who comes in to become part of the American mix. Because music is a product made by people for people, the sounds of music depend on the sounds of a people's musical language, the sound resources people can tap, the audience to whom music is intended to "speak," and the circumstances surrounding communication through music. If Irish music was not heard in the nineteenth-century living rooms and concert halls of the elite white Protestant society, social factors were more likely than musical ones to account for the absence.

That there was no evidence of Mandarin-language Beijing opera in nineteenth-century America becomes understandable in light of who the early Chinese were who came to the country: they were Cantonese-speaking immigrants who would have patronized Cantonese—not Mandarin—opera.

Since the nineteenth century, the Irish and Chinese immigrant experience has been repeated, with varying degrees of effort and success, by immigrants from all over the world. But it is important to remember that underlying a successful new growth in the vast field of American musical diversity is the climate and the quality of the soil in which it must take root. These are defined not by musical factors alone but by political, economic, and broadly cultural factors as well.

It surely is not a coincidence that at a time when the 2000 census is showing Latinos on the verge of becoming the biggest minority group in the United States, Latin popular music, which used to be a niche market, has now entered the American musical mainstream. The larger society's reception of performers such as Ricky Martin, Christina Aguilera, and Carlos Santana, and the sales of these artists' recordings, attest to it. And while it is in the popular music arena that Latin American music is best known to American audiences at large, composers with Latin American roots are making their presence increasingly felt in the art music field.

Take "Batey" (1991; CD track 12: excerpt from the "Rumba" section), for example, which Tania León wrote in collaboration with Michel Camilo. It is performed here by the Western Wind vocal ensemble, with Daniel Ponce playing the *conga* (an Afro-Caribbean one-headed cigar-shaped drum hit with the hands), Erik Charlston and Joseph Passarro on percussion, and conducted by Tania León.

León was born in 1943 Havana, Cuba. She was trained as a pianist and earned the equivalent of a master's degree in that country before coming to the United States in 1967. She became accompanist, music director, and subsequently resident composer of Arthur Mitchell's Dance Theater of Harlem and conductor of its orchestra. She has a doctorate in composition from New York University and was New Music advisor to Kurt Masur when he was conductor of the New York Philharmonic Orchestra. She founded "Sonidos de las Americas," a program that brought dozens of Latin American composers to New York City, many of whose works were performed in Carnegie Hall. Her collaborator, Michel Camilo, is a pianist and composer born in the Dominican Republic with a command not only of Latin American music but of jazz and art music as well.

"Batey" is a word said to have been coined by West African slaves to refer to the village that housed those who worked on sugarcane plantations. The piece, written for six amplified singers and six percussionists, who play an array of traditional and nontraditional instruments, has a text that is "primarily Spanish but . . . embraces nonsense syllables [vocables], a few words of English . . . and Yoruban, and what León calls 'a Cuban dialect that imitates the dialect of Africanos'" (Schwartz 1994: 13).

The "Rumba" segment in CD track 12 displays an unmistakable Afro-Caribbean rhythmic flavor. It employs an organizational principle common in that part of the world as well as in parts of West Africa: a repeated rhythmic pattern that anchors the musical activity swirling around it. The pattern can be played on drums, cowbell, or hardwood sticks or *clave*. In the "Rumba" it is played prominently on drums.

ACTIVITY 2.6
Listen to the clave in the background. It is audible at the beginning of the segment, and you can get used to its sound before the voices come in a few seconds later. Keep track of the rhythmic pattern played on it and you will hear clave patterns that you will hear again in a different context later.

Listen for the drum pattern played almost to the end of the segment. Clap or tap it. When the pattern has become familiar, clap or tap it with the music. You may want to try having someone improvise on an object or instrument with a different timbre as you repeatedly tap the rhythm, the way the drums in "Batey" anchor the vocal parts and the improvisatory layer played on a higher-pitched drum.

Bring to class examples of Latin music where some of the same features can be heard.

The changes in the American musical landscape brought on by the immigration reforms of 1964 and 1965 accelerated in the final quarter of the twentieth century. The rise of such formerly unheard-of musical genres as Asian jazz and Korean rap would hardly have been possible were there no sizable Asian American population out of which makers and users of such genres would come. Similarly, the proliferation of so-called ethnic musics: they pour out of restaurants to match the featured

FIGURE 2.3   *The Asian Garden mall in Westminster, California, where Asian stores proliferate and where the architecture combines the functional character of the American mall and Chinese decorative features.   (Photo by Adelaida Reyes.)*

cuisine. Music for worship runs the gamut, from that performed in storefront churches to that heard in cathedrals, synagogues, mosques, and temples. Concerts and performances of music from all parts of the world have become commonplace. Instruction on many of these musics can now be had in conservatories and music departments where, until the mid-twentieth century, the curriculum was dedicated exclusively to Western European music. Students take lessons so that they can become musically multilingual. There are radio programs dedicated to ethnic music of one kind or another. Ethnic festivals proliferate, topped by the big one that brings musicians and dancers from all parts of the United States to the National Mall in Washington, D.C., during the summer.

The musical ideas and influences do not flow in one direction only. Immigrant musics borrow as much as they are borrowed from. The critic Jon Pareles notes a ska rhythm from Jamaica, the sounds of a North Indian sitar and tabla, the Brazilian samba beat, and "a keyboard line fit for a techno track" in the Puerto Rican singer Ricky Martin's music

(1999:1). Jennifer Lopez injects rhythm and blues elements into her Latina music making. And give-and-take between African American and Euro-American musical techniques and sensibilities has animated jazz throughout its evolution.

Authenticity, in the sense of the faithful reproduction of music as heard in its original contexts, has not been the concern of those in the popular music and art music fields. In these areas, musics from other cultures are more likely to be seen as resources rather than as objects for cultural conservation. They are therefore adapted to serve different functions. Sound and context are inevitably altered. *The King and I*, the Rodgers and Hammerstein musical based on Margaret Langdon's novel *Anna and the King of Siam* (now Thailand), freely simulated "oriental" elements with no pretense at being authentically Thai. Listen, for example, to "Prayer to Buddha" from the musical *The King and I* (Angel Records 7243 5 27351.2.9), which has nothing in common with Buddhist chant. (See Wade, *Thinking Musically*, on orientalism.) Cross-fertilization, stimulated by diversity even as it, in turn, stimulates diversity, follows almost inevitably from close encounters between musical cultures.

The long-term effects of immigration may lie less on the *ingredients* of the American mix than on the *attitudes* and *values* that shape American musical culture. Long after America declared itself an independent nation, its musical life remained so dominated by Western European values that as late as the 1920s it was still "an intoxicating notion that Americans could be composers without any help from Europe" (Sandow 2001). Until the mid-twentieth century, the best way to get a professional art music career launched in the States was via European credentials—European training or European acclaim or both. Given America's pluralist and egalitarian ideals, this long-lasting dependence on Europe for musical approval challenges full understanding until one looks at features of demography and immigration policy within a historical framework.

Even as the population grew in numbers, immigration policies maintained the Europe-derived majority by prohibiting or restricting the entry of non-Europeans through quotas. Until the 1950s, 80 percent of those immigrating to the United States were of European ancestry (Burkhead 1994: 581). Power—social and aesthetic—thus stood firmly on a Europe-derived base for more than a hundred and fifty years after the nation declared its independence.

It is of course true that immigration and demography alone do not determine what cultural values will prevail. In the case of a nation built on pluralist and egalitarian principles as America is, it is particularly difficult to find a clearly definable cultural identity that transcends multiple origins. Americans had to travel a long road through two world wars and earn status as superpower before they could take their independence from Europe as a *psychological* reality. Only then could they break free of their habitual deference to Europe.

It is also true that the reform of immigration laws in the 1960s widened the range of diversity throughout the country as nothing had before. In that decade, the black power and civil rights movements laid the groundwork for the rise of ethnic pride among African Americans, Native Americans, Latinos, and other groups. With the influx of Asians and formerly locked-out populations, diversity built up enough of a critical mass to mount a multiculturalist challenge to the then-dominant Anglo-European melting-pot assimilationist ideal. From the five categories of the 1790 census, which essentially divided the population into two—white (i.e., of European stock) and black—the number of categories in the 1990 census offered five major categories: white, black, Asian/Pacific Islander, American Indian/Native Alaskan, and other. In the 1990s, 90 percent of those who came to become Americans were non-European. By the 2000 census, the choice of categories to which one can belong racially and ethnically ballooned to sixty-three.

These developments saw the growing ambiguity of cultural and racial boundaries as conditions increasingly favored testing and crossing boundaries over trying to dissolve them. Hybridity in all its forms and musical sources worldwide now flourish in an environment where European immigration no longer dominates. An unprecedented number of musical hybrids have come into existence. They now seem poised to become the rule rather than the exception.

ACTIVITY 2.7

Look back on your collection of music that you began classifying at the beginning of this chapter. See if you need to re-consider in which group specific items should go. Then select what you consider the best example from the group representing diversity through the infusion of imported musical elements and the best example from the group that you felt straddled the categories or groupings. In light of what you have learned about diversity thus far, discuss your choices. Point out what elements or influences were "imported" and from where. Explain why you put the "straddler" in that category.

If you have had difficulties deciding to which category or group some or all of the items belong, discuss those difficulties within the framework of American musical diversity and its sources.

Diversity from Within.   Nourished by a variety of cultures and brought up believing in individualism and its seemingly boundless choices, America has sometimes behaved like a child who spits out spinach only to sing its virtues as an adult. Americans have often ignored sources of diversity in its own backyard—the Africans and the Native Americans early in American history, for example. At other times, they have tried to eradicate differences in the crucible of the melting pot. But the nation, though periodically rebelling against them, and although unable to live up to them, has never cast off its root ideologies. In impressing upon the new nation the value of the egalitarian ideal, the Founding Fathers endorsed its logical consequences—inclusiveness and diversity. As principles, these were embedded in the American state (in its government) and the American nation (in its culture). As reality, they are manifested in the sturdy, self-perpetuating varieties of homegrown diversity that now dot the American landscape.

Diversity through Aggregation.   Diversity also increases when cultural units are added to an existing whole. In the twentieth century, for example, a great variety of cultural groups became part of the American scene when Alaska and Hawaii became part of the United States. The following examples give an indication of how the new Americans helped broaden the range of American musical diversity.

"Hello Song" (CD track 13) is by Nicholas R. Charles Sr., an Eskimo from Alaska. It recounts casual meetings with various people in the course of taking a walk. The singers, who sing in unison, are accompanied by a frame drum.

ACTIVITY 2.8
Listen to CD track 13.

(1) Focus on the text. Even if you do not understand the words of this piece, write down the text as it sounds to you.
(2) Shift your attention to the drumbeats. Put a mark above each text syllable where you hear a drumbeat. Note where the steady

drumbeats are interrupted. Using clues provided by the drumbeats, determine where phrases begin and end. If necessary,
rewrite the text so that each phrase begins on a new line.
(3) Look at the visual representation of the piece while you listen
to it, and describe its form. If you can, extend your listening
and analysis to other elements in the piece.
(4) Following the same steps, listen to CD track 1 and analyze
the form of the piece.
(5) Based on your analysis of the two pieces, compare them in all
their features (meter, rhythm, pitch range, etc.; see Wade,
Thinking Musically) and especially in their form.

Hawaii, the state that is thousands of miles removed from the American mainland and itself a group of islands, contributes to American
culture a diversity of its own. Chinese, Filipinos, Koreans, and Japanese are among those who, along with Americans from the mainland,
have settled in Hawaii over the last few centuries.

The Polynesian base of Hawaii's culture is exemplified by "Aloha e
ke kai o Kalalau" (CD track 14). This is a *mele* (chanted poetry), a traditional form that is treated with great respect. It is considered personal
property and is passed down like an heirloom from one generation to
the next.

In this item, the *mele* is accompanied by a drum (*pahu*) that is never
used as a solo instrument. It has a wooden body and a sharkskin drum-
head that is struck with the hands.

ACTIVITY 2.9

Compare the melodic range of this song with the previous song
(CD track 14). Compare the drumming and the way it is used
as accompaniment to the text. Discuss the use of the drum in
each case.

Look back on your analyses of CD track 1 and CD track 13.
On the basis of musical features alone, can you say that those
two songs and this Hawaiian sample come from the same musical culture? Discuss the reasons for your response to this question.

Diversity through Divergence from Common Roots. Other varieties of homegrown diversity emerged not as a direct result of appropriating elements from other musical cultures but by diverging from the music makers' own cultural and musical roots. Of this variety, the work of Harry Partch (1901–74) is exemplary.

Partch exemplifies the idea of diversity internalized and reincarnated. The son of missionary parents who served for ten years in China, Partch was surrounded by things Chinese. Many boyhood years spent in the Southwest made Mexican and Yaqui Indian music familiar to him. His exposure to different cultures was supplemented in adulthood by a year-long research trip to England, where time spent reading in the British Museum and a meeting with the Irish poet W. B. Yeats added up to what has been described as a formative experience. For his compositions, his source material ranged from Greek tragedy to Japanese *nō* drama to African stories.

Partch's interest, however, was not in collecting musical sounds from different cultures. His energies as a composer were targeted toward challenging the traditions of the Western European musical world, from its concertgoing practices, to the division of labor between composer and performer, to its system of pitches and hence to the tuning of musical instruments. What he extracted from his experience of diversity was a sense of what is possible outside the Western European tradition. And the possible is what he made actual in the service of his musical mission, which he articulated in 1942: "I have been provoked into becoming . . . a musical apostate. . . . My devotion to our musical heritage is great—and critical. I feel that more ferment is necessary to a healthy musical culture. I am endeavoring to instill more ferment" (Partch 1991: flyleaf). Here is a quintessential individualist, an energetic frontier pusher, identifiable as an American type. These attributes show through in the examples on CD track 15 ("U.S. Highball") and CD track 16 ("The Letter").

The instrumental sounds of "U.S. Highball" simulate train sounds—the whistle, the wheels against the rails, and so on. To produce them, Partch used instruments that he himself constructed from found materials. He gave his instruments names like Diamond Marimba, Bass Marimba, Spoils of War, and Boo (all percussion); Kithara, Castor and Pollux, and Surrogate Kithara (strings); and Chromelodeon (an "adapted reed organ") (Partch 1991: 212). The instruments were designed to deviate from the pitches of the Western diatonic scale: instead of dividing the octave into twelve equal intervals as the Western musical system does, Partch divides the octave into as many as forty-three different pitches. This allows him to notate the finer nuances of human sung or intoned speech.

FIGURE 2.4 *Harry Partch's Boo, a bamboo marimba with six rows of tuned bamboo tubes open at both ends and played with a pair of mallets. Bill Ruyle plays Boo II, recently renovated.* (Photo courtesy of Bob Vergara, APS.)

The central character in "U.S. Highball"—the hobo—is about as familiar to Americans as the cowboy or the self-made man. The text or libretto of "U.S. Highball," which follows the cry, "Leaving San Francisco, Californi-o," with which CD track 15 ends, is a complex combination of what the protagonist (the hobo, in an early version called Slim and later, the Subjective Voice) thinks and the remarks of those around him. They are simultaneously reflections of what is going on in the protagonist's head and what the others actually say; of what goes on in the freight car and what goes on outside as the train moves from one state to another. There is no linear narrative.

The voice that recounts the hobo experience and intones "The Letter"(CD track 16) straddles speech and song in a manner that is closer to today's rap than it is to European opera recitative.

In Partch's work, the emancipation of an American's music from that of Western Europe is, if not complete, well on its way to being so.

Although the struggle for American musical autonomy continued for the better part of the twentieth century, clear signals that it was eminently achievable came from the work of American-born composers such as Charles Ives (1874–1954) and Henry Cowell (1897–1965) early in the first half of the century. These composers led a rebellion against the way books then said music should be written—against the rules of the Western European musical system. The following are examples of the way that rebellion sounded.

From his adolescent years, Henry Cowell was an enthusiastic explorer of music's possibilities. He used fists and forearms on the piano to produce tone clusters before these were introduced in Europe by composers like Bela Bartók. A noted teacher and pioneer, Cowell tirelessly promoted composers he considered undeservedly unsung—among them, Carl Ruggles (1876–1971) and Charles Ives—using his book *American Composers on American Music* (1933) and the *New Music Quarterly*, which he edited, for that purpose.

In "Banshee" (1925; CD track 17), Cowell's only concession to the Western European tradition is the grand piano, the instrument for which the piece is scored. His use of the instrument, however, was thoroughly unconventional for the time. Someone sits on the piano bench but never touches the keyboard. His or her function is simply to keep the damper pedal (the one that the right foot depresses) down for the entire duration of the piece. What this does is lift the dampers that otherwise lie on the strings, thus allowing the strings to vibrate freely. Someone else stands beside the piano to pluck or to slide fingers across the strings. With the strings undampened, the sounds bleed into each other and the effect simulates the wailing of a banshee (a spirit in Gaelic folklore who "cries" to warn that death is near).

Charles Ives, the son of a small-town bandleader, was steeped in music from childhood. Surrounded by the sounds of music as it was being performed all around him, he began composing at a young age. He became a highly successful businessman, in no small part so that his composing—a life-long avocation—would never have to be compromised in the face of financial pressures. This independence shows in his music. Like Cowell, Ives reveled in breaking the formal rules of composition.

This spirit bursts out mischievously both in the sounds he concocts and in the words he uses to describe what he had in mind for "The Gong on the Hook and Ladder" (CD track 18). He sets the scene: the annual parade of the neighborhood volunteer fire company in which the carriage drawing the hook and ladder marched slowly on a route that went uphill and downhill. The gong behind it was supposed to ring "steady-like," but when the carriage went downhill, it rang fast, and when it went uphill, it rang slowly and thus did not quite stay in step with the band. "Nobody always seemed to 'keep step,' but they got there just the same" (Ives quoted in Sachs 1986).

Individual innovators like Cowell and Ives represent the internally generated diversity of American music particularly in the realm of classical or art music. The energy and the sheer exhilaration of innovation comes across as being very American in its individualism and pioneering spirit. But these innovators never intended to produce a unitary musical system or a musical school of thought with its own recognizable musical identity. What they contributed was a declaration and an unmistakable show of independence from Western Europe—a strong statement of what their music was not, what it need not be, and hence, what departing from the European model could potentially be.

As contributions to American musical diversity, therefore, the sound of classical or cultivated music written by American composers in general occupied a gray area. As a product of European training, heavily if not completely reliant on European modes of expression, American art music was often accused of being more European than American or of being European and not American. In the first quarter of the twentieth century, those in search of an American sound turned either to jazz and popular song or, as in the case of European concertgoers, to music like Charles Ives's, which "had not been diluted by European training" (Griffiths 2001: 40).

This situation was inevitable in light of the fact that the system of musical education in schools was based on the Western European musical system, a consequence of the historical and demographic factors described earlier. This was therefore the system that was transmitted institutionally from one generation to the next. The embeddedness was deepened by musicians who went to Western Europe for further musical training. And the arrival on the scene of some of Europe's greatest musicians during World War II reinforced what earlier pro-Europe immigration policies had established and sustained.

Diversity in Motion: Redrawing Boundaries. The distinct voices of cultural diversity therefore had to come, at least initially, from the margins of the musical scene. The rise of ethnic identity in the 1960s moved the musical cultures of immigrant communities out of the shadows. Multiculturalism created a climate highly conducive to the formation of the modern equivalent of the Founding Fathers' factions. There are now groups whose musical identities derive primarily from what they have in common socially—from their gender, for example—or from the musical repertories they promote; hence, groups like the Lesbian American Composers, the Gay Men's Choruses found in many cities, early music groups, and twentieth-century music groups. But large-scale internal migration—population movements within the country's borders—deserves special mention for its wide-ranging effects on American musical life.

Recall that diversity, in the early days of the nation, was a matter principally of regional and ideological differences. The lines defining those differences were fairly clear and were reinforced when people stayed in place, within a community of like-minded members. When people move, they adapt to new environments; allegiances are likely to shift and boundaries to give way.

Large-scale rural-urban migration brought about an explosion of interest in folk music nationwide shortly after World War II. Songs gathered earlier in the twentieth century in relatively isolated locations by collectors like John and Alan Lomax enriched the repertories of latter-day singers and balladeers like Pete Seeger, Jean Ritchie, and Paul Simon and Art Garfunkel, who in turn adapted the materials to urban audiences.

"Goodnight Irene" (CD track 19), for example, was one of some five hundred songs recorded by the African American blues singer and guitarist Huddie Ledbetter (1885–1949). Also known as Leadbelly, he was discovered in a southern prison by the Lomaxes, who supervised the recording of Leadbelly's songs when he was released on parole. "Goodnight Irene" subsequently entered the urban folk and popular music repertory.

"Scarborough Fair" as sung by Paul Simon and Arthur Garfunkel (from *Simon and Garfunkel's Greatest Hits*, Columbia CK31350) is a more recent example of the way folksongs are transformed in urban contexts. Originally an English ballad sung and rediscovered in Appalachia, it was performed traditionally as an unaccompanied solo (listen, for example, to Pete Seeger singing "Barbara Allen" on CD track 30). Pete Seeger popularized a homophonic version, accompanying himself with a guitar in a style similar to that with which he sang "Yankee Doodle" (CD track 2). Simon and Garfunkel's version is thoroughly urbanized, produced with the help of electric and electronic technology, featuring complex polyphonic textures, and with an urban audience in mind. Ballads from Appalachia, cowboy songs from the West, hillbilly songs from the white rural South, and blues from the Mississippi Delta found new life and were similarly transformed in cities.

The most important of the internal migrations that eventually redrew regional, racial, and musical boundaries was that of African Americans.

FIGURE 2.5   *Huddie Ledbetter (Leadbelly).*   *(Courtesy of the Library of Congress, Prints and Photographs Division, Reproduction No. LC-USZ62-120591.)*

Beginning as a trickle in the early twentieth century, it gathered momentum as the century wore on and peaked shortly before World War II. The chain reactions that the migration set off as it moved from the rural South to cities such as Chicago and New York culminated in the transformation of jazz and of American perceptions of jazz (to be discussed in more detail in chapter 4).

After World War II, popular music gained momentum and transformed itself from a mere purveyor of music that sought a common denominator into an active promoter of the new, spurred on by commodification and a market that is continually in search of novelty.

People have enthusiastically embraced the "age of everything. . . . Open-mindedness rather than any single sound was [the 1990s'] great contribution: a lesson in diversity. . . . [F]rom a fan's perspective . . . the decade of grunge, hip-hop, women in rock, a resurgent Nashville, teenybop and Latin pop was remarkably fertile, accommodating a different trend seemingly every year" (Weisbard 2000: 1). In hip-hop, originally thought of as African American and male, one now finds Latino, Jewish, Asian American, and female performers. The South Asian diaspora has joined the world of hip-hop with performers like Panjabi MC, introducing Indian instruments, Indian film music and dance tunes to the mix. This will surely not be the final development.

ACTIVITY 2.10
Search the Web and listen to the radio for rap music and talk about rap.

Make a list of these: titles/topics; name and gender of rapper; language(s) used; musical instruments used; and other features you consider significant.

Based on your findings, draw a picture (in words) of the rap scene you have witnessed, speculating on how it reflects American musical life and culture in general.

But perhaps more to the point is the growing fluidity of the lines that are intended to separate genres and musical types. Some writers and marketers have sought to cope with the resulting confusion by making finer and finer distinctions. In his book *Generation Ecstasy*, Simon Reynolds (1998) counts more than forty genres of techno and rave that include New York Garage, Terrorcore, Horrorcore, and Ambient Techno. Rock had been through this before as it spawned hard rock, soft rock, punk rock, and so on. But the result has fed rather than ended the confusion. Musicals become acclaimed as operas. Popular music composers write concertos and have their works performed by virtuosos in concert halls. Electronic music, once thought of as the domain of "serious music" and the relatively few who had access to sophisticated sound laboratories, has resurfaced as popular music's electronica. Increasingly, generalizations about music genres or musical types flirt with meaninglessness.

In the meantime, technology speeds up the blurring of lines that distinguish the effects of immigration from those of internally generated diversity. No longer dependent on the physical presence of immigrants, who were their carriers throughout history, musical ideas now arrive from all over the world through the media. Decontextualized and detached from the people who had subjected them to the rules of a musical and cultural system, musical ideas and materials now become free agents. Thus unbound, they become vulnerable or receptive to exploitation, manipulation, appropriation, hybridization, and a wider range of creative possibilities. Like their predecessors, who came as part of human migration, those musical ideas and materials transform the American landscape as they themselves are transformed by their new environment.

DIVERSITY AND THE AMERICAN MUSICAL SCENE

Does all this indicate a descent into chaos? Perhaps what the Nobel prize–winning scientist Murray Gell-Mann has to say about complexity is worth invoking, for Gell-Mann is an authority on the subject, and the American musical scene is surely one of the most complex in the world.

According to Gell-Mann, two attributes are embedded in complexity: the chaotic and the simple. The simple is linear: a cause leads to an effect. Chaos is nonlinear. It seems random and arbitrary. But one needs the other in complex systems. There must be enough order to preserve some continuity. And there must be enough disorder "to jolt species . . . forcing them to innovate or perish" (Ferris 1995: 41). Throughout the chapter there have been signs of the randomness and arbitrariness that seem to spell chaos. But I submit that they are signs not of anarchy or deterioration but of the "ferment" that Harry Partch saw as an enhancement to survival and identity, a necessary ingredient for leavening and invigorating a culture. In the ensuing chapters, the emphasis shifts to the sources of coherence and continuity that counterbalance diversity's centrifugal tendency to spin out of control with the centripetal power of order to hold a system's diverse parts to a core.

CHAPTER 3

Identity and American Music

> *Do I contradict myself?*
> *Very well then. . . . I contradict myself,*
> *I am large. . . . I contain multitudes.*
>
> —*Walt Whitman*, Leaves of Grass *(first edition, chant 51, lines 1314–16)*

In one of the greatest American poems, and with just a few master strokes, Walt Whitman (1819–92), one of America's most celebrated poets, gave us a most concise, beautifully drawn American self-portrait. In it are contained realities that underlie ages-old American problems of identity. And in it, we catch a glimpse of attitudes toward those realities that are peculiarly American.

The "I" here is not Whitman, the individual, but a stand-in for a collective identity, for an American every(wo)man marked matter-of-factly by internal conflict. Twice in the space of three short lines, the words "I contradict myself" appear. That statement is met not with hand-wringing anguish but with an almost casual "Very well . . ." Whitman's use of the present tense is prophetic; almost a century and a half after *Leaves of Grass* (1855), the self-contradicting character is alive and well, embodied in a "nation of nearly 300 million notoriously contentious souls" (Kennedy 2002: WK3).

The self-contradictions and inner conflicts that both plague and animate American life are the inevitable consequence of the primacy that America has given the individual while building pluralism into the system. Within a democratic framework and in the context of what the eminent psychologist Erik Erikson called a "once-in-history chance of self-made newness" (1974: 60), pluralism created an undreamed-of wealth of options. With it and the unprecedented freedom to carve an identity at will came the dilemmas of choice and the anguish of uncertainty. The penchant for newness awakened a longing for identity's rootedness; the need to assert individuality tugged at the desire to be part of a com-

41

munity. These oppositions breed the condition that Erikson claimed to be almost native to the United States—a condition that he called identity crisis and attributed largely to emigration, immigration, and Americanization.

As far back as the early 1800s, Alexis de Tocqueville, in his much-translated two-volume classic *Democracy in America*, saw opposition in all aspects of American social life. Deeply religious sentiments were interwoven with highly materialistic aspirations, individualism with a strong tendency to join associations, pragmatism with idealism. The contemporary belief that internal tension is "the very essence of American character" (Ledeen 2000: 166) goes back almost to the time of the country's birth.

Are the self-contradictions and the internal tension evident in American musical life as well? If they are, what part do they play in shaping American musical identity? A look at two songs can open the door to a discussion of the first question and serve as prelude to exploring the issue of identity in the American musical context.

A STORY OF TWO SONGS

"God Bless America" (CD track 1) by Irving Berlin (1888–1989) and "This Land Is Your Land" (CD track 20) by Woody Guthrie (1912–67) are songs about America written by Americans, in a musical idiom familiar to virtually all Americans. Both were composed in the second quarter of the twentieth century. Both became American anthems. But each projects an image of America that differs markedly from the other.

Both songs are written in the diatonic system that dominated Western European music in the late eighteenth and nineteenth centuries. The meter is a straightforward marchlike duple, and both songs use a typical four-line strophic form. The relation of text to tune is syllabic (one syllable per pitch), and the lyrics of both songs are in English.

Where external features are concerned, therefore, the two songs are made from the same mold. But their message—the America that each song projects—are in opposition. This is made clear in the text. Berlin's America is a cloudless, expansive Utopia:

> *God bless America,*
> *Land that I love*
> *Stand beside her, and guide her*
> *Through the night with a light from above.*

From the mountains
To the prairies,
To the oceans, white with foam
God bless America, my home sweet home.

Guthrie's America was overcast and restrained. It was a vast and beautiful land but it was not paradise. Guthrie's lyrics painted personal observations of a wall keeping the well-off separate from the down-and-out; of a line of hungry people outside the Relief Office. Where we now hear "This land is made for you and me," Guthrie had initially written "God blessed America for me." There were a number of versions, the one heard in CD track 20 being the authorized version, but parts of the original were used in performance by Woody's son, Arlo, and by Pete Seeger.

> **ACTIVITY 3.1**
> *Like Woody Guthrie, Harry Partch also hoboed for years in the 1930s, during the Great Depression. Compare the music and the text of "U.S. Highball" and "This Land Is Your Land," both of which come out of the two men's experience as hobos at about the same time in the country's history. Note and discuss the insights you get into how and why representations of the same landscape can be so different from each other.*

But, one might argue, the opposition is expressed in the words. How can these songs be *musical* illustrations of the opposition that is central to American identity?

There are answers to this question that are rooted in the nation's history and will become evident as we proceed. For now the question can be addressed by looking into the relation between the songs' words and music. We can then see whether the songs as such—not just their tunes or their lyrics—can be taken as a pair in opposition.

It is not unusual for a tune and the lyrics of a song to have lives independent of each other. Poems might be set to a tune that long has had an existence of its own. Melodies initially composed for musical instruments may subsequently be converted to song through the addition of words. But there are songs that their listeners know only as songs, their words and music like Siamese twins, virtually inseparable from each other. This is the case with both "God Bless America" and "This Land Is Your Land." To my knowledge, neither song has had its words set to other tunes. Nor has the tune of either song been used for words other than those the composer had written for them. But these circumstances by themselves are not conclusive. Those surrounding the songs' creation carry far more weight.

"God Bless America," introduced on Armistice Day in 1938, came into being out of Berlin's desire to create a morale-boosting number at a time when the country was being shaken by the war in Europe which did escalate into World War II the following year. Guthrie's "This Land Is Your Land," originally titled "God Blessed America," was composed specifically to challenge the image of America painted by Berlin's song. In an interview broadcast on National Public Radio on September 3, 2000, Guthrie's daughter Nora told the folklorist and program producer Nick Spitzer that her father's reaction to "God Bless America" was: "Who is blessing America? What America is being blessed?"

Each composer, therefore, intended tune and text together to express his own view. That the title and the line "God blessed America for me" was subsequently replaced by "This land was made for you and me" does not change the meaning and sentiment embedded in Guthrie's song. Over the years, despite the songs' opposite visions of America, Americans seem to have respected each composer's intended text-tune union: neither tune has been used for a different text, and neither text has been set to a different tune.

All these factors—the composers' intent and the American public's apparent endorsement of the unity of text and tune—allow us now to compare the songs as an opposing musical pair.

The resemblance in the external features of the two songs, and their common status as anthems, throw their differences into sharper relief. "God Bless America" is a prayer, addressed to an abstract being. "This Land Is Your Land" is a secular statement addressed directly to the American people. "God Bless America" is a timeless vision. "This Land Is Your Land" is a time-bound image, informed by a specific period in the country's history, although Guthrie, judging from his daughter Nora's remarks, did not intend it to be so. The version that launched each song dramatized the contrast between them. "God Bless America"

FIGURE 3.1 *Woody Guthrie. (World Telegram photo by Al Aumuller. Courtesy of the Library of Congress, Prints and Photographs Division, Reproduction No. LC-Usz62–113276).*

as performed originally by Kate Smith was sung with full instrumental ensemble, in a voice and manner that would not have been inappropriate on an operatic stage. "This Land Is Your Land" was sung by Woody Guthrie accompanying himself with an acoustic guitar. It is as self-accompanied solo that the song is best known to audiences.

In both songs, the fit between the work, the circumstances of the composer's life, and the particular vantage point from which each viewed his subject endowed the songs with notable integrity. Berlin's patrio-

FIGURE 3.2 *Irving Berlin (center) with Richard Rodgers (left) and Oscar Ham-*
merstein II, watching hopefuls who are being auditioned on the stage of St. James
Theater on Broadway, New York City. (World Telegram photo by Al Aumuller, 1948.
Courtesy of the Library of Congress, Prints and Photographs Division, Reproduction No. LC-USZ62-
126707.)

tism—he would be awarded the Congressional Medal of Honor for his
services to the U.S. Armed Forces during World War II—combined com-
fortably with his unabashed affinity to Broadway and Tin Pan Alley
(New York City's music business center). In Berlin's arena consumer
tastes and commercial interests played a prominent and unapologetic
role. This was the milieu of composers and lyricists like George and Ira
Gershwin (*Porgy and Bess* [1935], *Lady Be Good* [1924], *Funny Face* [1928]
An American in Paris [1928]), Cole Porter ("Begin the Beguine" [1934],
"I've Got You under My Skin" [1936]), and down the line to Richard
Rodgers and Oscar Hammerstein (*The Sound of Music, The King and I*),
and Frederick Loewe (*My Fair Lady*). Guthrie's realm was that of urban
folk music, where great value was placed on "keeping things real."

There, the luminaries were balladeers like Pete Seeger, Arlo Guthrie, and Joan Baez.

ACTIVITY 3.2
Listen to either "Do, Re, Mi" or "My Favorite Things" by Richard Rodgers and Oscar Hammerstein from the album The Sound of Music *(RCA 07863). Compare it to Woody Guthrie's "I ain't got no home" (CD track 21). Pay particular attention to the nature of the subject matter, the potential "consumers" of each song, the form and the instrumentation. Do you see any parallels between your comparison of this pair of songs and the Berlin and Guthrie comparison? Specify the commonalities and the oppositions.*

Both Berlin and Guthrie exerted a powerful influence on other songwriters. And as for American society as a whole, one can almost hear them say with Whitman's "I" and just as casually: "Very well then . . . I contradict myself." The opposition of God and Mammon, of the world governed by the spirit and that governed by material wealth, are thrown once again into sharp relief.

Opposition, then, does not subvert a common identity in the American context. Rather, it is at the center of identity definition. Opposition and the tension it generates are to be maintained more than they are to be resolved. Taken singly, "God Bless America" and "This Land Is Your Land" each gives individuals an America of their choice. Americans can, as Guthrie and Berlin did, and as Erik Erikson implied, envision their own America. Taken together, however, as a pair in opposition, the two songs make a stronger statement about America than each by itself can make. Jointly they demonstrate the internal tension born of opposition that scholars, artists, and observers of the American scene have found at the core of American character. It is a tension reflected in what Ann Powers has written of rock 'n' roll: "born at a violated boundary—between white and black, rural and urban, commercial and folk. . . . [It] thrives on the confusion of the busy crossroads" (Powers 1999: 45). With only slight modifications, the description can be applied to rap, to jazz, to composers who write and conduct symphonies and just as comfortably write finger-snapping, ethnicity-flavored songs and dances for Broadway musicals. It is what the former Living Color guitarist Vernon Reid must have had in mind when he noted that the positive collision of values is what's made American culture (Fricke 1999).

The constant ferment and tension that opposition brings to American life gives it an emergent quality—more concerned with self-renewal or reinventing itself than with completing itself. In the American musical scene, process competes with product, experimentation with the tried-and-true, image making with self-discovery. The American sense of self, and of music as an expression of that self, is a perennial work in progress. In an environment such as this, identity becomes a crucial issue.

IDENTITY: FROM THE GROUND UP

Derived from the Latin *idem* ("same"), the term *identity* emphasizes sameness or equivalence. We identify *as* someone or something, *with* those with whom we have something in common—our nationality, race, religion, ideology, to take the most commonly used grounds for identification. And when we identify something—a person, an object, a piece of music, a group of persons or objects—we are pointing out what that entity has in common with others in the same group. A protest song, for example, is identified as such according to a set of features that it shares with other protest songs. Difference is part of the definition, of course, but it functions primarily as trigger. It prods one to identify oneself when there is an other from whom one wishes to be distinguished. Difference, therefore, while essential, is ordinarily left unsaid. Identity expresses the grounds for belonging.

The diversity of America's population, however, has turned the spotlight on difference. As more and more people from different backgrounds and ethnicities come to become American, and as more and more groups insist on an identity of their own, identifying oneself has become a matter of who one is *as different* or *distinct from* someone else. In the American multinational, multicultural nation-state, difference wrestles with sameness or commonality to hold the key to identity. Identity as a matter of defining a self, of expressing who or what one is, competes with identity as a means of defining an other, of expressing who or what one is not. When difference gains the upper hand the very notion of an *American* identity or character tends to be either dismissed or met with skepticism. It is then that people say that American identity is an illusion. Up close and in the short term, heavily dependent on who or what one is not, identity takes on a quicksilver quality that makes it seem impossible to capture.

Yet evidence that there is such a thing as an American identity is everywhere. The oft-repeated phrase "Only in America . . ." suggests not just geography but also a widespread and collective sense of distinctiveness, social and cultural.

ACTIVITY 3.3

Complete this sentence every way you can think of: "Only in America can one [hear, see, do, etc.]." Narrow the subject down to "Only in America can music be . . ." Compare your sentences with those of your classmates. Do you find a consensus or general agreement on what makes America and American music unique?

In light of what you have read thus far and of the insights you have gained from the sentences you and your classmates have written for this activity, write an essay of no more than three hundred words on the subject of American (musical) identity. As with the results from your other activities, keep this essay and see how your thoughts have evolved thus far and how they evolve as you read on.

That American identity stands for something recognizable is corroborated by the acknowledgment that things can be "un-American." Can one pin down that recognizable something? Picking apart the concept of identity and examining three elements that play an important part in its construction—the human dimension, markers of identity, and context—is an essential first step.

The Human Dimension.   If everyone belonged to the same tribe, family, clan, or human group, by whatever shared features that group may be defined, there would be little or no incentive for group identification. The same holds true for assigning identity to objects. Identity, as the social anthropologist Fredrik Barth noted, comes into being when people perceive difference and find it significant enough to require articulation (1969). This perception raises a boundary that separates those who belong together and those who do not. This is how the distinction between self and other, as individuals or groups, as we and they, as ours and not-ours, this and not that, comes into being. The members of "our group" and "their group" may change, as may the pieces that constitute "our music" or "their music"—"Yankee Doodle," after all, might once have been "theirs" and is now claimed to be "ours." But the boundary that ensures the distinctness of ours and theirs, of one thing and some other, remains.

Ideally, identity is unambiguous: there should be no mistaking who one is or what something is. But identity, especially in the American context, can be fuzzy (as by now the activities have made you aware) and variable for reasons already noted. Distinctions can become insignificant. Grounds for differentiation lose their clarity or change too fast to be spelled out with any accuracy. Jon Pareles, the *New York Times* popular music critic, for example, decided that rock in the 1990s had become "a polymorphous mess . . . encompassing hip-hop, dance music and the rest of the mess" (1993: AR1). The boundaries of sound and style that had kept them separate had lost much of their function and significance; the boundaries of human interest had taken over to justify affixing different labels.

To identify clearly, therefore, *people* must perceive difference, and they must see the need to make that difference recognized. Without people, identity is as meaningless as dots in a pointillist painting that has no viewer to give those dots meaning.

ACTIVITY 3.4
Listen to CD track 22, "Gray Goose," sung by Sweet Honey in the Rock. (Other musical items may be used.) Identify it any way you can—by title, type of music (popular, folk, classical, rock, blues, etc.), national origin (Irish, Chinese, etc.). Note why you identified the piece as you did. If you named the piece by its title, it is probably because you know the piece, in which case you identified it in the strict sense of sameness (idem): it matches the original piece of that name. The identity is unambiguous. You have also set up a clear boundary differentiating it from other songs.

> *If you have* not *identified the song by name, compare your responses with those of your classmates and, with them, select the responses that best reflect how and on what basis people assign an identity to something, exemplified in this activity by a piece of music. Discuss the role that people play in assigning identity— the knowledge, impressions, predilections they bring to it; their need to make distinctions; and so on. Compare the level of ambiguity in the identity based on a clear, absolute standard (being the same as an original) and in the identities assigned on variable personal, social, intellectual, and other bases.*

Markers of Identity.   Identity requires markers—tangible things that people use to signal difference or distinctiveness, things that signify something other than themselves. Sometimes they are permanent, like birthmarks or fingerprints. Sometimes they are impermanent like a password or a code name. A flag or a jingle or a logo serves as marker for the identity of a nation, a commercial product, or an organization, respectively. But until they are assigned their function by convention, habit, or law (i.e., human agency), they have no power to represent. Thus, "The Star Spangled Banner," which began life in the eighteenth century as a British drinking song, did not become an official marker of national identity until 1931, when Americans adopted it (with patriotic text written by Francis Scott Key in 1814) as a national anthem. (Hitchcock 1969: 28).

> **ACTIVITY 3.5**
> *Surf the media (TV, radio, the Internet). Select a jingle or musical logo or piece of music that serves as marker for a particular product, group, or institution. Describe the music. Describe the group, product, or institution for which it is being used as a marker.*
> *Speculate on who the prospective listeners/buyers/subscribers are intended to be. Make a case in writing or orally for why the music is or is not effective as a marker in terms of the match between the music, product, group, or institution and the targeted*

FIGURE 3.3   *Two of the most common markers of American identity: the Statue of Liberty and the American flag.*   *(Photo by Adelaida Reyes)*

audience. In your presentation, include any other factor you can think of that allows a piece of music to function as a marker, that is, to identify a person, group, or thing.

An example of a musical marker of ethnic identity is the *clave*, a term that refers to a rhythmic pattern played over and over in the course of a piece. (The term also refers to the instrument that plays the pattern—a pair of hardwood sticks struck against each other). Heard by itself or as part of an ensemble, it is immediately identifiable as

FIGURE 3.4 *The clave pattern (from Gershwin's* Cuban Overture*), which can also be heard on CD track 24.*

Latino, or more specifically, Afro-Caribbean, by those who identify themselves as such.

The most distinctive of such patterns can be heard on CD track 23 (*Cuban* Overture [1932]). Used by the piece's composer, George Gershwin, as marker of his composition's Cuban-ness, it is notated for what Gershwin calls "Cuban Sticks" as shown in figure 3.4 (other musicians notate the pattern as beginning with the second measure).

The power of this marker was demonstrated at one of the summer concerts sponsored by the city of New York and performed on the streets. The performance—this one in a predominantly Latino part of New York City—was just winding down, and the large crowd on the street was responding with hearty applause, which continued even as the musicians started packing up their instruments. Suddenly, someone picked up a bottle and, with his car keys, began playing the rhythmic pattern shown in figure 3.4. In no time at all, the crowd picked it up, clapping the rhythm or playing it on whatever they could use—car fenders, mail boxes, fire hydrants, soda cans. The growing wave of sound engulfed everyone. Out came the musicians' instruments once again, and before long a jam session of Latin popular music was rocking the stage. The street burst with new life as people danced. The clave as emblem of shared ethnic identity had been used effectively to acknowledge, acclaim, and ask for more of what musicians and audience knew as *their* music.

I was not able to record the event described above. But at another concert featuring Tito Puente and his orchestra, a similar incident occurred (CD track 24).

ACTIVITY 3.6
If you have a recording that features the clave pattern, or one to which the pattern can be added as a complement, share it with your classmates and discuss its function in the piece. Does it serve as a marker of Cuban or Latino ethnicity?

FIGURE 3.5   *A street concert in New York City similar to the one described in the text.   (Photo by Adelaida Reyes.)*

Context.   Identity as a label assigned to people or things, and identification—the way identity is assigned—almost always change with context.

ACTIVITY 3.7
Note the different ways people are asked to identify themselves (e.g., Who is it? in response to a knock at the door. Or, Who should I say is calling? Or, Who do you think you are?).

1. *Create three columns. In the first column, enumerate different forms in which the question "Who are you?" can be asked. In the second column, note the occasion for each form of the question. In the third, note what you think is an appropriate response in each case.*
2. *Discuss how items in column 3 are affected by items in the other two columns. What would happen if you rearrange the responses*

in column 3 so they no longer correspond with the context (column 2) and the form of the question that goes with it? Try scripting and enacting an individual case, and discuss the results.

"We Shall Overcome" (CD track 25, as sung in 1964 at a Hattiesburg mass meeting in Mississippi) was originally a Christian church hymn. C. A. Tindley, who became America's first important African American gospel songwriter, had written it for his congregation. In the 1960s it was adopted by the Civil Rights Movement and became an anthem

FIGURE 3.6   *Civil Rights march on Washington D.C., August 28, 1963.*   *(Photo by Warren K. Leffler, U.S. News and World Report Magazine Photograph Collection. Library of Congress Reproduction No. LC-U9-10363-5).*

associated in the minds of the nation with the African American struggle for equality and freedom from discrimination. In the 1970s it became a rallying cry in the fight against drugs being waged by the Latino and African American population of New York City's East Harlem. Its strophes sung alternately in English and Spanish, "We Shall Overcome" helped redraw boundaries, erasing those based on ethnic differences. Latinos and African Americans put their shared identity as members of the East Harlem community ahead of their ethnic identity to stand united in the fight against drug lords and drug users in their community. This was significant: on other issues such as funding for English-as-a-second-language programs, the boundary was clearly drawn with the Latino and African American groups occupying opposite sides of it.

In 1996, at an American Thanksgiving Day celebration in Oxford (United Kingdom), what the same song symbolized underwent another transformation. In the presence of other Americans and guests from the local and international community (mostly Europeans and Africans), one Anglo-American after another stood up to describe their connection to the Pilgrims. Then an African American began to sing "We Shall Overcome." Immediately, the other guests who knew the song joined in. In no time, the one voice had become a rousing chorus.

I hazard to guess that when he began, the singer had intended the song to call attention to his difference from the earlier speakers and to the fact that, though American, he, as an African American, had no connection to the Pilgrims. As the other Americans joined in, the song assumed new meaning. The emphasis shifted from the difference that the African American singer was signaling to the shared meanings that "We Shall Overcome" has for all Americans. Finally, as the non-American guests added their voices, the scope of the song's meaning expanded beyond the boundaries of one national ideology. The non-Americans may just have been joining in on a party activity. But they may also have been expressing solidarity with the African American individual who initiated the singing in the narrow context of that Thanksgiving celebration. Alternatively, they may have been expressing solidarity with what he stood for in the wider context of racism and universal human rights.

Here, then, is a song that began life as a Christian hymn intended for use in church. In different contexts, it assumed new functions, marked different identities, and itself assumed different identities. It became, in turn, an African American anthem, an East Harlem rallying cry, and a song for human rights that was not specific to nationality or region. Through it all, it remained unchanged as a piece of music—in its form, its content, and its tune.

IDENTITY ON THE NATIONAL LEVEL

Much of what has been presented above applies as much to individual as to national identity. But there are constraints on the construction of national identity that call for separate treatment.

Communities, by definition, are built on what their members have in common. As a community grows in size and internal diversity, common understandings and common features tend to decrease in number. While there is therefore virtually no limit on what markers individuals can use to identify themselves as they respond to immediate and changing contexts, the limits on the markers a nation can use are considerable. Markers of national identity must be recognizable and acceptable to constituent members over a long period of time; they cannot be changed every month or every year. And for America, they must stand for the identity of what Walt Whitman had called "a nation of nations," culturally diverse but one nation nonetheless. National identity, whether ascribed to a culture or to a music, thus tends to be expressed in broad generalizations that focus on common denominators even and especially as the nation's members and their products grow more diverse.

When Jimi Hendrix, for example, took America as subject matter for a famous performance in Woodstock in 1969, he needed a long-standing, nationally recognized symbol that leaves no room for ambiguity. "The Star Spangled Banner" was one of the few markers that filled that bill.

The first few seconds of music were enough to let the audience know what song Hendrix was referring to; when he began to alter the anthem, the audience easily surmised that what the anthem customarily stands for was likely to be altered too. Hendrix molded the music, bending the tune this way and that, flying off on tangents, embellishing the musical events with all kinds of sound effects—wailing, groaning, police siren-like sounds that are highly resistant to conventional musical notation. After the musical line to which "And the rockets' red glare" is usually sung, for example, he plays what can be described as the musical equivalent of "Whee-eee!" Periodically he returns to a phrase or two of the anthem's tune as though to remind the audience of the subject matter of this performance and, as he resumed his deviations, to highlight his divergent view of what the anthem stands for.

In the context of that time and place, in a decade when America, racked by internal conflict, was doing a lot of soul searching, the America of Hendrix's "Star Spangled Banner" was obviously not the America of the national anthem. Nor was it Irving Berlin's or Woody Guthrie's America. Strictly through music, without the use of lyrics, he made clear reference to America, but not the America of his time, rather of "the next America" (Fricke 1999). It was, in the words of the former Living Colour guitarist Vernon Reid, "Martin Luther King's 'I Have a Dream' speech on guitar" (ibid.).

ACTIVITY 3.8

Find a recording of Hendrix's "Star Spangled Banner." Listen to the whole piece and draw a schematic diagram as follows:

1. *Write down the text of "The Star Spangled Banner."*
2. *To facilitate later comparison, use a stop watch or the timer on your CD or tape player to indicate the point in time at which you hear a segment of the original anthem. Underline or highlight the part of the text that is usually sung to it.*
3. *Compare your findings with those of your classmates. If there was consensus or unanimity in the findings, these points in the music were functioning efficiently as marker of Hendrix's subject matter. In other words, at those points, everyone knew that reference was being made to the national anthem and what it stands for.*
4. *Describe the special effects and musical "commentaries" that Hendrix put in between these segments. Would you consider these markers of national identity? Why, or why not?*
5. *Toward the end of the piece, Hendrix quotes "Taps," a tune used in camps to signal lights out at the end of the day. It is also used in funerals, probably as marker to signify the end of a life. Recall occasions when you have heard "Taps." Discuss the use of "Taps" in the instances you remember and speculate on Hendrix's use of it. Was he using it as a marker? If so, for what?*

The processes by which a symbol can be made to stand for a national identity, both actual and imagined, calls for more than musical analysis. They are perhaps better served by analogy, using a parallel instance in which those processes are clarified by language use. For example, "my fellow Americans" is a form of address that, over the years, American presidents have used to identify themselves with the nation. One is hard put to find a label that is more inclusive and generalizing. None so effectively shifts the focus away from the huge differences in individual identities and national origins that the label encompasses. So when Franklin Delano Roosevelt, one of the most popular of American presidents (in office from 1933 to 1945), chose to ignore that form of address in a speech to an indisputably American organization, opting to call his audience "fellow immigrants" instead, questions of appropriateness quickly arise.

First, the members of the organization, the Daughters of the American Revolution (DAR), did not consider themselves immigrants. Qualification for membership in that organization required proof of an ancestry that goes back to someone who had supported the American Revolution. By their definition, the DAR members were descendants of the first Americans.

Second, Roosevelt was not an immigrant in the strict legal sense of the term. He belonged to an old American family and his wife was legitimately a Daughter of the American Revolution. Roosevelt, therefore, had even more reason than when addressing the nation as a whole to call the DAR "fellow Americans."

But what seemed anomalous on the face of it was in fact a well-considered choice. The DAR had been drawing criticism for its discriminatory policies. These came to wide public attention when the DAR barred the celebrated African American singer Marion Anderson from performing in their hall. It had not mattered that Anderson was acclaimed all over Europe and hailed by the great conductor Arturo Toscanini as a "once-in-a-century phenomenon." Mrs. Roosevelt resigned her membership in the DAR in protest. She then backed Ms. Anderson's historic performance at the Lincoln Memorial in Washington, D.C., the site where, some years later, Martin Luther King Jr. was to galvanize the nation and the civil rights movement with his "I Have a Dream" address.

In light of these events, Roosevelt's identification as immigrant became a far more significant choice than "fellow Americans" would have been. Recalling America's self-identification as a nation of immigrants,

FIGURE 3.7 *Marion Anderson broadcasting a Negro spiritual at the dedication of a mural installed in the United States Department of the Interior building, commemorating the outdoor concert that she gave at the Lincoln Memorial after the Daughters of the American Revolution refused to allow her to sing in Constitution Hall.* (Photo by Gordon Parks. Courtesy of the Library of Congress, Prints and Photographs Division, Reproduction No. LC-USW3-013421-C.)

Roosevelt chose to underscore his identification *with* immigrants and, symbolically, *as* immigrant. In the process, he managed simultaneously to define Americanness in ideal terms as an all-inclusive nation, while rejecting the reality of the DAR's exclusive and segregated America.

This, in effect, was what Hendrix had done in his version of "The Star Spangled Banner." Confronted by the limited number of ways by which Americanness can be unequivocally expressed or evoked, both

Roosevelt and Hendrix took nationally recognized markers, so that even as they abbreviated those markers and reshaped their use, what they were referring to was never in doubt. At the same time, the America they were referring to was an America in conflict with itself—as envisioned and as present-day reality.

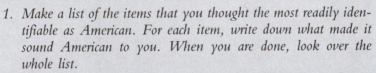

ACTIVITY 3.9
Listen again to the CD tracks discussed thus far. Try to find recordings of the compositions so that you can listen to them in their entirety.

1. *Make a list of the items that you thought the most readily identifiable as American. For each item, write down what made it sound American to you. When you are done, look over the whole list.*
2. *Comparing your results with those of your classmates, discuss what markers, characteristics, or features pointed most directly at an American identity. If you could not find any or if you could not agree on any, discuss what the reasons might be, using this chapter's discussion of identity as point of reference.*

Summing Up. What defines identity is first and foremost the boundary created by perceptions of sameness and difference that must for some reason be expressed. But it must always be kept in mind that boundaries are movable, redefinable. The identity that boundaries define is seldom absolute—hence, recently invented labels such as pan-Indian and pan-Asian, which did not exist before the twentieth century.

People communicate or decipher identity through markers—tangible things like labels or logos or pieces of music. Markers can be replaced; company logos, signature tunes, and flags are periodically updated. A single marker can be varied to alter its meaning, as the Hendrix example has shown. Or without changing in form, it can change in function and in changing contexts, as "We Shall Overcome" has demonstrated.

These fundamentals provide a much-needed anchor in the turbulence, complexity, and excitement of the American scene. They keep in perspective the potential for fragmentation that diversity brings while keeping real the concept of unity that American national identity demands.

THE SEEDS OF COMPLEXITY: THE GENESIS OF AMERICAN MUSICAL BOUNDARIES

The seeds of American identity were sown when the new country declared its independence from its European forebears. That event put colonials on the road to becoming Americans. But the new identity was not to be an organic growth from common soil. It was not to be, as in the European nation-states, the outcome of shared language, beliefs, customs, traditions and norms. The new nation, as Edward Rothstein has put it, echoing others before him, "may be the only nation in the world that was invented from an idea, lacking any foundation in a defined territory, a religious authority, a common culture or a single people" (2000: 21). The choice of markers for the new nation's cultural identity, therefore, promised to be contested and highly problematic. Philip Gleason, in the article "American Identity and Americanization," which he wrote for the *Harvard Encyclopedia of American Ethnic Groups*, explained:

> A sense of distinctive peoplehood could be founded only on ideas . . . because the great majority of Americans shared language, literature, religion and cultural traditions with the nation against which they had successfully rebelled and from which they were most determined to establish their spiritual as well as political independence. The non-British minority did not offer a language, religion or common culture upon which the national identity could be based. (1980: 31)

The Native Americans, who preceded the colonialists in the New World, themselves comprised separate nations. Each had a language and culture of its own. Until 1871, when congressional action ended the practice, those nations, their sovereignty recognized, could separately negotiate treaties with the U.S. government. Thus it was highly unlikely that support for an overall American national identity could have been constructed on a Native American base.

The situation that Gleason described, earlier referred to by Erik Erikson and reaffirmed by Rothstein, had an enormous impact on musical identity or on the expression of cultural identity through music. Lacking referential meanings, and by nature highly ambiguous, music could not effectively express its separateness from Europe while using the language and the system that were the most important markers of European musical identity. In the young American nation, therefore, medium and message were at odds. How then was American music to differentiate itself from its European parents and establish an identity of its own?

F. L. Ritter's *Music in America* (1883), the first comprehensive work on the American musical scene, exemplifies a response common at the time. He simply sidestepped the issue. Perhaps more accurately, he did not see an issue. His was a perspective shaped by his European background. His expectations were conditioned by the common Old World view that a nation's music is governed by one musical system in use by a people who shared a culture with deep roots in a common past. Music in the Western European musical idiom was automatically European. Thus, despite American and African American music everywhere, Ritter reported an "utter absence of national . . . music in America" (quoted in Chase 1966 [1955]: xvi). Works now considered wholly American such as Stephen Foster's "My Old Kentucky Home," "Oh, Susanna," (CD track 9) and "Swanee River" (CD track 26) or the marches of John Philip Sousa (1854–1932) (CD track 27) could not, in the view prevailing at that time, be American. This was the case with ragtime as well (CD track 28), which was then gaining in popularity. Where musical multilinguality in a single national identity was inconceivable, message-medium, form-content discordance would not be an issue.

The virtual nonexistence of American musical identity was thrown into sharp relief by a vibrant American literature where the inherited verbal language, English, was being used to project a distinctly American identity. By the time Ritter's work appeared, Ralph Waldo Emerson and Henry David Thoreau had already been recognized as authentic American voices. In 1885 Walt Whitman joined Emerson and Thoreau in the American literary pantheon with the publication of *Leaves of Grass*. American literature was giving abundant evidence of the uniqueness that Tocqueville had recognized and celebrated in his brilliant two-volume work *Democracy in America* (1835, 1840).

For American music, lack of referential meaning and the expectations born of the experience of the European nation-state were not the only obstacles to creating or locating a boundary that would distinguish it from European music. Unlike the independence of the United States, marked unequivocally by the American Revolution and the Declaration of Independence, the very idea of American musical independence took more than a century even to rise to consciousness. This was due in no small part to the resistance of the new Americans to assigning other-

FIGURE 3.8   *John Philip Sousa, leader of U.S. Marine Band (1880–92) in navy uniform, marching at the head of his bands during World War I.*   *(Defense Department photo (Marine Corps). Courtesy of the Library of Congress, Prints and Photographs Division, Reproduction No. LC-USZ62-104900.)*

ness to those to whom they were still bound by deep historical, cultural, and personal ties. America thus chafed against but nonetheless emulated those whose cultural hegemony it found difficult to escape. And even as those ties were loosened by time, there remained the fact that the principal threat to identity is not what one differs from most obviously but what one resembles enough to be mistaken for.

The recognition of a boundary that distinguishes America's music from other musics, Europe's in particular, was the necessary prelude to formulating an American musical identity. But it was slow in coming,

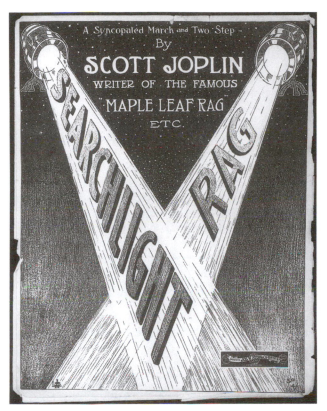

FIGURE 3.9   *Cover of Scott Joplin's "Searchlight Rag" (1907).   (Item No. Music B-424. From the Historic American Sheet Music Collection, 1850–1920. Rare Book, Manuscript, and Special Collections Library, Duke University.)*

and its full emergence was to be delayed further by the growing complexity of American life. Industrialization, the arrival of immigrants from an expanding circle of nations, and the blurring of class lines, to mention only the more obvious factors, challenged the location and the nature of the identity-defining boundary. New points of view were needed to sort through and find order in this rapidly evolving environment. Perhaps the most important one was provided by ethnomusicology, which was born as the nineteenth century was about to turn to the twentieth.

Particularly as it came to be practiced in the United States, ethnomusicology sought to release the study of music from the strict confines of sound. It argued for inclusion in the definition of music, the human behavior that went with the creation and use of music as acoustic phenomenon. It insisted on the social and cultural contexts from which music draws its meanings. Music, seen in light of this redefinition, broadened the field in which the boundaries separating ours and not-ours, the musical self and the musical other, can be found.

The new perspectives introduced by ethnomusicology were to have special relevance to fundamental issues of American musical identity. For when music is seen as cultural artifact and social act, its characterization can reach out beyond sound to a wider social environment for markers of its own identity. The burden of musical identity need no longer be borne by musical sound alone.

Gilbert Chase, the American music historian, was among the first to see the ramifications of this new way of looking and listening. "By America's music," he wrote in the first edition of *America's Music: From the Pilgrims to the Present*, "I mean the music made or continuously used by the people of the United States, people who come from many parts of the earth to build a new civilization and to create a new society in a new world" (1955: xxi). This statement is striking both for what it requires and for what it does not require of what Chase would call "America's music." It requires a primary and prominent role for people as makers not only of music but of the culture and society that is its context. It does *not* require a unitary musical system—a single musical language that would create a monolingual American musical life.

Richard Crawford, writing in his introduction to the third edition of *America's Music* (1987), took this to mean that for Chase, "the key to American music lies *in the nature of American society*" (xi; emphasis added). Chase, Crawford writes, was "the first general historian of [America's music] to recognize [it] as a unique phenomenon" (xv) and "a cultural statement" (xvi). Crawford continues:

> [T]he essence of American musical life . . . lay . . . in the complexity and disorderedness of the whole—in short, in the *discontinuities* of the New World's musical life with the Old. It is precisely in the author's perception of America's *difference* from Europe that the viewpoint of *America's Music* is rooted (xv; emphases in the original).

These words give evidence that the long and hard struggle for recognition of the boundary between Europe and America had finally been won, although echoes of the battle continued to reverberate until the late twentieth century. The charge that work of American composers was an imitation or appropriation of European music surfaced periodically. Hence, to the last decade of the twentieth century, Gilbert Chase and his successors continued to support the proposition "that writers of American history should explore and dramatize differences between this country and Europe" (Crawford 1993: 34).

A BACKWARD GLANCE

Today, in the twenty-first century, the belief that a national musical identity springs from a single primordial culture has been eroded. It has been challenged by an American musical life that is a composite of different cultures, each of which is allowed both to partake of American identity and to retain its own. Cultural diversity and other sources of difference have assumed a prominent role in the drama that is American identity construction. But the "I" of American identity is, as Whitman has noted, large enough to accommodate a multitude of diversities. It is an "I" that is ceaselessly under construction, reenacting in ever changing contexts the tug-of-war between those elemental opposites, the self and the other. Identity construction is an interplay of who or what one is and who or what one is not. It is an interplay of perceptions: how the self sees the other and vice versa, and how those perceptions get translated into behavior. In the range of choices that American society offers, and in the underlying ideologies that people use to justify their choices—freedom, democracy, free enterprise, and individualism—identity emerges and assumes a distinctly American cast.

CHAPTER 4

E pluribus unum

Out of many, one. The American motto speaks as much of achievement as of aspiration. It declares that something has been created: early in American history, people from diverse cultures began to come together to become one nation. It also announces a mission: oneness or unity is a continuing task, a work in progress, a living, evolving concept and not a finished product. One of the country's symbols, the unfinished pyramid, the central figure in the official seal adopted by the U.S. Congress in 1782, is still imprinted on the back of the American one-dollar bill. This sense of incompleteness and continual unfolding marks the perspective from which America's oneness is about to be examined.

The basis for national identity, oneness, is part of the bedrock upon which a nation stands. But it is not rigid. It must respond to social, cultural, and historical forces if it is to survive. Its face and its sound—its external manifestations—are mutable. In this respect, American oneness is no different from that of other nations. But in the conditions out of which oneness must be created and maintained, American oneness stands apart. The speed of change, the value placed on change, and the change-inducing elements that are built into the American political and social system obscure oneness often to the point of invisibility. As reflection of a people united, with a culture of its own, oneness seems particularly elusive in the American context. It is important to understand why lest we, as many have, entertain the notion that oneness or unity in American culture, musical and otherwise, is no more than illusion.

ONENESS: THE HISTORICAL DIMENSION

In the last chapter, we caught a glimpse of the long and arduous road America has had to travel in defining its musical identity. America's history, born of a conflict between a deep attachment to Western European culture and a rebellion against the British socio-political system, had left indelible marks on the nation's musical psyche. The fruit of that conflict—ambivalence—was a formidable barrier that stood in the way of envisioning oneness. Until the nineteenth century, more than fifty years after the Declaration of Independence, the historian John Higham has noted there remained a distinct hesitancy among the people to call themselves a nation (2001: 24).

In time, however, Americans realized that the first step to cultural independence was differentiation from Europe. The evolution of Uncle Sam as an American national symbol is a vivid example of how this realization was acted upon. Uncle Sam, John Higham reports, began life as a "blank, featureless male" who was tall and thin only because the British national type, John Bull, was short and fat (2001: 41). It took fifty years worth of alterations before he became the figure the world unequivocably associates today with the United States.

The historic conflict between European roots and rebellion against it, and the expectations of musical homogeneity raised by the concept of nation-state, made the task of musical identity construction peculiarly American. It elicited varying degrees of commitment from different sectors of the American musical milieu. Aaron Copland, for example, worked energetically on behalf of a distinctively American music. But the response of his fellow composers as a whole was unenthusiastic.

In 1926 the respected composer Roger Sessions advised Copland to stop " 'wasting precious energy' on anything 'so vague and dubious' [as American music]" (quoted in Tomassini 1999: AR36). Copland's contemporary Virgil Thomson said that one need only be an American and then write whatever music he or she wished. The farthest Copland got in mobilizing his colleagues to promote the cause of American music was to have them agree to an American composer-run organization. This ended up addressing not matters of sound and message but issues of royalties, performance, and subsidized publication.

Art music composers in particular ignored the ambiguous identity that their compositions projected through their use of the Western European musical idiom. Thus, until late into the twentieth century, music of Western European derivation continued to contend with the charge that it was either an imitation or an appropriation of the music from which it meant to be distinguished. In the 1990s the historian Gilbert Chase and his followers still felt compelled to argue for the need to differentiate American music from European music.

FIGURE 4.1   *Aaron Copland.*   *(Photo by Margery Smith. Courtesy of the Library of Congress, Prints and Photographs Division, Reproduction No. LC-USZ62-103702.)*

The persistence of these problems in the American context, however, did not come solely or even mainly from what American composers failed to do. It was rooted deep in the country's history.

Even in its infancy, the country was aware of the diverse cultures within it and of the different languages—musical and verbal—that were in use. Its response to this diversity was exclusion. While acknowledging three major populations—the European, the Native American, and the slave—the Constitution awarded the rights of liberty only to the Europeans. For almost a hundred years, only whites could become citizens. And despite changes in official policy, the sentiment persisted. In

Israel Zangwill's play *The Melting Pot* (1909), which popularized the term "melting pot" and put it in common use, the following lines appear in act 1: "America is God's crucible, the Great Melting Pot where *all the races of Europe* are melting and reforming. . . . God is making the American" (emphasis added).

The dominance of the former Europeans thus perpetuated Western European musical hegemony in American musical life. It became the musical language taught in schools. As late as the middle of the twentieth century, the music of two of America's largest minorities, that of African Americans and Native Americans, continued to be treated separately, essentially as the music of an other with an identity of its own.

Inevitably, however, this state of affairs could not stand without being challenged by the country's principle of pluralism. As people from different cultures began to populate the States, musical monolinguality based on Western European standard practice came under increasing pressure. But the primacy of musical monolinguality would die hard. African American music, for example, despite its widespread use—from dance floors to concert halls, from streets to churches—and despite its recognition as American in Europe, had to wait until the middle of the twentieth century for the social stigma to begin gradually lifting. Only then would its innovations on musical language become acceptable as American. It would take years more for the doors of academia to open and admit African American music into school curricula. Today, the study of Native American musics and the music of other minorities, not as autonomous wholes but as parts of a multilingual American musical culture, is coming into its own.

THE LANGUAGE OF ONENESS

The successful projection of an American identity in literature as early as the first half of the nineteenth century dramatizes music's difficulty as a medium for communicating national identity. It does not have verbal language's capacity for referential meaning. Music, therefore, cannot articulate, as verbal language can, American separateness from Europe, a prerequisite to creating and then asserting an American identity.

Aaron Copland and A Lincoln Portrait.   When the American composer Aaron Copland (1900–1990) meant there to be no mistake about who and what he was portraying in his composition *A Lincoln Portrait* (1942; CD track 29), he resorted to verbal language. Using words by and about Abraham Lincoln, Copland used some of the most quoted statements on what the United States stands for. It is a nation "conceived in liberty and dedicated to the proposition that all men are created equal." It is a democracy—"a government of the people, by the people, and for the people." Deliberately, the composer did not set these words and the rest of the text to music. He assigned the part to a Speaker, who may or may not be a musician. People such as Marion Anderson (a singer), Eleanor Roosevelt (former First Lady), Edward Kennedy (a U.S. senator), and James Earl Jones (an actor) have taken on this role. Paul Moore, a writer on music and friend of the composer, highlighted the significance of Copland's decision to use speech rather than song. Copland, Moore noted, "never resorted to words when he felt he could better express something in music" (n.d.: 7).

ACTIVITY 4.1

Find a piece of music that incorporates speech (spoken, not sung) into the composition.

1. *Look into the circumstances of the music's creation—the stories, if any, behind how and why it was written. Find out as much as you can about the composer's times and social environment, and about what he or she was trying to communicate.*
2. *Discuss or debate the merits of having the text spoken instead of sung in this particular piece of music. Support your argument: (a) by using only musical considerations, (b) by using the information you have gathered as evidence, or (c) by using both.*
3. *Summarize the insights gained concerning the efficacy of music as a medium for communicating ideas and images.*

In patriotic songs, the best markers of American identity remain their words. Tunes for American and European songs could not only be ambiguous, they could be identical. That is the case with the national anthem, which used to be a British drinking song, and "My Country 'Tis of Thee," whose melody is the same as the British "God Save the King." In songs like those of Bruce Springsteen, the lyrics, perhaps more than the nationality of the composer and performer, make unmistakable the American content of the music.

"My Hometown" by Bruce Springsteen. Over the years, Bruce Springsteen, one of America's best-loved singer-songwriters, has given his audiences perceptive sketches of America in song. A college dropout, he has nonetheless earned an honorary doctorate, and his works have become the subject for analysis and criticism in academia. But other people do the abstracting. Springsteen himself stays close to the ground, singing about working people who, in doing their jobs, become his heroes. He puts them in the context of current events. The police, firemen, and the nameless participants in the epic of New York on September 11, 2001; the shooting by police of the innocent immigrant Amadou Diallou as he tried to enter his apartment building; the Vietnam veteran whose experience of the war sets fire to "Born in the USA": these are the people Springsteen writes and sings about. Like the eye that Woody Guthrie casts on his country, Springsteen's is not complacent. Through the narratives and commentaries that are his songs, he holds up a mirror to his country, showing what there is to celebrate or calling attention to the ways it falls short.

"My Hometown" (Columbia CK 67060; available in at least 5 other albums) is the story of a town's decline from one about which the singer's grandfather, in happier times, would say, "Take a good look around, this is your hometown," to one that he is compelled to leave. Repeating the words "your hometown" or "my hometown" insistently in the song's refrains, Springsteen seems to suggest that this town could well be yours too. In quick strokes, he alludes to a place associated with childhood and remembered with fondness; a town like many other industrial towns in the country. Like many of them, his hometown suffered from racial tensions and the loss of jobs in the factory where many residents had worked. As he leaves with his family, he repeats to his son, with a touch of bitterness, the words his grandfather had often uttered with pleasure and with pride.

ACTIVITY 4.2.
Try to find complete recordings of "My Hometown" and "Born in the USA" so you can get the full story from the text and better relate the singing style to each story.

1. Study the lyrics. What is each song about?

2. Study the music without the lyrics. Determine the form of each song. Identify other musical features that would help you describe the music.
3. Contrast the singing style that Springsteen uses for each song. How would you account for the difference?
4. In each of the two songs, what best expresses what the song is about—the words? the tune? Springsteen's guitar playing? the singing style? What does each contribute to the song as a whole?
5. Write a comparative essay based on your answers to the above points.

The oneness that instigates national identity has thus been slow in coming both to the culture as a whole and far more especially to music. Historical events that shaped and continue to shape the nation, as well as the very nature of music, with its built-in capacity for ambiguity, account for that slowness. But like the depths of a great river, oneness is profoundly still and not easily accessible. It is the river's surface that calls attention to itself with the continual changes that are its response to outside forces—the wind, the tides, and the elements. The task of recognizing the underlying unity in America's music thus promises to be formidable—impossible, in fact, if one limits oneself to the observable surface, to music as sheer sound. For as that very American composer Charles Ives wisely remarked, "what [music] *sounds* like may not be what it is" (1962: 84; emphasis in the original).

THE PARADOX OF MUSICAL ONENESS: ITS CHANGING FACE, THE UNCHANGING MISSION

It is paradoxical that one cannot speak of American oneness without reference to American diversity. But America's unity is constructed from its differences—what they consist of, the way they are reconciled and oppositions between them resolved, the compromises along the way. What shows as the face of oneness thus differs accordingly.

In the early days, for example, when only former Europeans were entitled to become American, diversity was largely religious and regional. Problems arising from religious differences were resolved on the national level by the creation of two of the main pillars of American ideology. One, freedom of religion, subsequently became freedom of expression. The other is the equally continually reinterpreted principle of the separation of church and state. America continued to be religious, but the practice of religion was consigned to a space of its own. America defined itself as a secular society. Unity was secured, paradoxically, through the separation which defused the potential divisiveness of contradictory religious beliefs.

Regional differences were attenuated by spatial separation and resolved through mutual accommodation: the New England Yankee and the Southern plantation owner, for example, both became regional stereotypes. "Dixie" and "Yankee Doodle" both came to be considered American songs. The face of American oneness was secular and Caucasian, and the sound of its music was derived from the musical language—and even the repertoire—of Western Europe. In addition to "Yankee Doodle" and the British drinking song that became "The Star Spangled Banner," a large body of British ballads are now considered American folk songs (e.g., "Scarborough Fair," "Barbara Allen"). They serve as reminders that, particularly in the realm of folk and traditional music where authorship as ownership is not as contentious an issue as it is in art music, such imports can become American through convention and association. (Remember that African Americans and Native Americans were excluded from the definition of American.)

"Barbara Allen" is a ballad, traditionally understood to be a song that tells a story. There are many versions or arrangements of "Barbara Allen," a few of them with American copyrights. But the basic song, now considered American, is of either English or Scottish origin. In the Pete Seeger rendition sung on CD track 30, the song is performed without accompaniment, the way English ballads were traditionally sung as a form of storytelling.

ACTIVITY 4.3

Analyze the form of "Barbara Allen." (Writing down the lyrics line by line makes the form more quickly discernible.)

Describe the melody and the text-tune relations.

Refer to Thinking Musically, *especially activities 4.13 and 4.14, and see if the melody can be accompanied with the basic chord progression described, the way most American folk songs and traditional ballads can be.*

Compare the musical features (form, text-tune relations, musical language, etc.) of "Barbara Allen" with those of "My Hometown" and "Swanee River" (CD track 26). Based on the results of your comparison, construct an argument for or against "Barbara Allen" being American rather than English or Scottish.

Two world wars and the September 11, 2001 attack on New York's World Trade Center were dramatic demonstrations of how external threat can drive America's sense of unity out into the open. Divergent populations that under other circumstances would profess different loyalties metaphorically and actually rallied around the flag. Differences—cultural, racial, ethnic, religious—were forgotten as voices from the entire cultural spectrum joined in to sing and create patriotic songs. "God Bless America," which had been created on the eve of World War II, was, according to a *New York Times* poll, the most frequently sung anthem in the days following the 9/11 attack. New songs have begun to appear: Toby Keith's "Courtesy of the Red, White, and Blue," Neil Young's "Let's Roll," and Bruce Springsteen's "Into the Fire." But the fervor that pushes unity into the forefront of national awareness tends to cool with the passing of the crisis that induced it. Unity retreats to its accustomed place: out of sight.

Oneness, made complex by the principle of pluralism and not readily observable, might thus be best demonstrated through the two greatest challenges to it and the observable forms that were the nation's response to those challenges. First is the greatest threat to oneness posed by race. The measure of its disruptive force is the Civil War that nearly destroyed the Union. The other is the huge influx of cultures from all over the world that resulted particularly from the immigration reforms of 1964 and 1965. The first had deep roots and bore bitter fruit. The full impact of the second is yet to be felt.

Multiculturalism and Oneness. Cultural hybridity is like its biological counterpart: the more closely related the participating cultures are, the more likely the success of the union. When the European colonials became Americans, the Scots, British, Germans, French, and so on, more easily found common ground than do the contemporary Chinese, Africans, Mexicans, Vietnamese, and so on, who are in the process of becoming Americans. Among early Americans, the problem was one of differentiating themselves as Americans from their forebears. Their music and that of their European "parents" were so similar that they were difficult if not impossible to tell apart. In the case of contemporary non-European Americans and formerly excluded American populations like the Native American, the problem lies in bridging huge cultural differences, and finding—or inventing—similarities on which to build a common identity.

"Caverns" by Jason Kao Hwang draws from different Asian musical traditions represented by the members of The Far East Side Band (CD track 31). Jason Kao Hwang is an American-born Chinese poet, composer, and free-jazz violinist who has written scores for the Public Broadcasting System (PBS), documentaries, and plays. In this recording, he performs on an electric violin. Yukio Tsuji, a Japanese-born composer and performer, contributes to the sound resources not only with Japanese instruments—bamboo flute (*shakuhachi*) and Japanese drums (*taiko*)—but with Native American shakers and Chinese and Turkish cymbals. Sang-Won Park, who was trained as a performer and musicologist in his native Korea and made his Western debut in Carnegie Hall in 1979, sings in the style of Korean folk opera (*p'ansori*) and accompanies himself on a Korean zither (*ajang*).

Contributing elements and ideas from their respective cultures and from their experience of other musics, the performers of "Caverns" assemble a rich palette of sounds, which they use to "paint" collaboratively. Sharing a reverence for nature and using jazz-inspired techniques of improvisation to come together, "Caverns" is less a music of tunes and chords (although they are there) than one that conjures colors and moving shapes in space and time. What pulls the different musical elements together is less an adherence to the rules of any of the musical languages from the participants' cultural heritage than to the ideas that motivate the sound events. These include the willingness to experiment, the freedom to do so, and the drive to explore beyond the confines of a single culture. These may well represent the ideas that Gleason had in mind when he wrote that America's sense of peoplehood can only be founded on ideas. They are specific to the individual artists involved; they can also be considered native to American culture.

ACTIVITY 4.4
Bring to class examples of p'ansori *singing, and of* shakuhachi, taiko, *and* ajang *playing as these are performed in their tradi-*

tional or accustomed contexts. (Recordings are available from big record stores, Japanese or Korean stores, your library, and possibly from downloads on the Internet.)

Listen to the sounds separately before listening to a recording of "Caverns." Then listen for the differences in usage and sound effects when they are used in combination in "Caverns."

Describe those differences. Do they detract from or support an American identity?

Like many modern American musicians, R. Carlos Nakai and AmoChip Dabney do not confine themselves to a single musical tradition. Nakai, of Navajo-Ute heritage, is a formally trained musician specializing in trumpet and music theory. His first musical language is therefore that of Western European derivation. Only in adulthood did he come to the Native American flute, driven to it by curiosity and learning to play it largely on his own. With his mastery of the instrument, he has explored its possibilities outside of the heritage to which it belongs. He has played with musicians from different musical cultures—Tibetan and Japanese among them. He has also founded an ethnic jazz ensemble and is well known for his performances of New Age music.

Dabney is of African, Native American, and European descent. He also has a conservatory background, with training in saxophone, bass, piano, and composition. He has worked with African American ensembles (Sun Ra and his Omniverse Arkestra), and African groups (the Nigerian All-Stars) and, like Nakai, wishes to explore the potential of his multiple heritages in the creation of music beyond specific cultural constraints.

In "Stomp Dance" (CD track 32) Carlos Nakai and AmoChip Dabney set out to investigate the way their respective musical cultures converge or diverge while exploring the capabilities of their instruments. The title of the composition refers to a Native American dance from the southeastern part of the United States. In the Native American context, it is performed by a line of dancers to music provided by singers and drummers. But creating music for the stomp dance was not what Nakai and Dabney had in mind. Nakai is explicit: his intent is "not to reiterate the traditional sounds but to find new avenues of expression for both the traditional and contemporary native cultures of America" (Nakai 2001). Dabney combines his interest in improvisation with serious attempts to understand the many musical cultures that are part of both his heritage and his experience in performing with groups from other cultures (ibid.). The result is a combination of features that are attributable to traditional sounds (e.g., the steady drumbeat, the sound of the Native American flute), and others that come from the artists' diverse and contrasting experiences as individual musicians.

Polyphony, which one hears in this piece, is not common in Native American music. Nor is the almost total dominance of melodic lines moving in parallel perfect fifths (see *Thinking Musically*). Song, an essential component of the stomp dance, is absent. The assignment of the melodic part of the stomp dance music to wind instruments departs from the form's conventions. In short, the search for "new avenues of expression" uses to advantage sound materials and concepts from distinct American cultures. It probes the differences between individual American musicians who started off from different points in the racial, cultural, and musical spectrum and ended up discovering ways to musical integration.

ACTIVITY 4.5

Find out as much as you can about the Native American stomp dance: what it looks like, what the music sounds like, the instruments used, the occasions for doing the dance, who performs it and for whom, and so on.

Add your own observations about how Nakai and Dabney's piece parts ways with the traditional stomp dance.

Formulate arguments for or against the Americanness of "Stomp Dance."

The face and sound of oneness differs not only according to the ingredients that are thrown into the mix but according to what American society as a whole makes of them. Until the twentieth century, the dominant metaphor for the country's response to the challenge was the melting pot, where differences would melt into a smooth blend with a European flavor. But as incoming populations became more and more disparate culturally, as resident populations chose to form groups with identities of their own (e.g., gender-based identities), and as minority groups increasingly took pride in their cultural origins, it became clear that cultural differences can be "unmeltable." Oneness as a smooth blend gave way to what the historian John Higham has called an "uncongealed amalgam" represented by new metaphors. Salad bowl, rainbow, mosaic all refer to ingredients or components that retain their integrity even as they combined to invent and reinvent a whole.

Multiculturalism gained prominence. Just as one did not have to speak English to become American, a musician, to be an American musician, did not have to be proficient in the Western European–based musical language of the majority. Fusions, crossovers, hybrids, and all forms of appropriation became legitimate—even desirable—options. Composers and performers felt free to pick and choose from whatever musical systems served their creative purpose. This is the musical equivalent of free enterprise, where musical goods can be introduced and traded at will. Boundaries defining genres or entire musical cultures are blurred or crossed without compunction. These practices, singly or in combination, are no longer seen as departures from the norm; they have entered America's musical mainstream.

One can now take off on Zangwill and his lines from the play *The Melting Pot* quoted earlier: America has become a crucible where cultures from all over the world come together to create an uncongealed amalgam. They are making the American.

Leonard Bernstein (1918–90), a Massachussetts-born composer, conductor, and pianist, took great pleasure in the freedom of musical expression that the new climate afforded. A classically trained musician, he composed Broadway musicals as readily, it seemed, as he composed symphonies. In his compositions, he drew from musical influences that ranged from his European-derived musical heritage to jazz to Caribbean rhythms, from secular as well as from religious sources. His Second Symphony has an extended piano solo, in itself unusual in the symphonic form but more so because the solo's idiom is unmistakably jazz. His fondness for jazz and Latin American music are much in evidence in *West Side Story* (a Puerto Rican–white American *Romeo and Juliet* that later became a movie). In his *Kaddish* Symphony, named after a Jewish ritual prayer, he paid tribute to his Jewish heritage. In *Mass*, a piece that defies classification and is called a theater piece, he combined dance with elements of folk music, rock, and blues; the sound resources of an orchestra in the pit, a band onstage, and choruses; liturgical texts in Latin, Greek, and English; and street clothes and ritual vestments for costumes. They are all tied together by the concept of the Roman Catholic mass in a manner that makes the celebration of that sacred ritual a secular form.

FIGURE 4.2 *Leonard Bernstein (right) with composer Stephen Sondheim in 1978.* *(From the Leonard Bernstein Collection. Library of Congress, music division.)*

Bernstein's was clearly not a melting-pot approach to the diverse musical resources at his command. In his hands, the different cultural elements retain their distinctive sound and flavor even as he gives them the stamp of his musical individuality. The process is reminiscent of the words of the writer Richard Todd: "To be an American means figuring out *how* to be an American. We are . . . *bricoleurs* in our own culture—we pick and choose, paste together, make it up as we go along" (2001: 16). (Coincidentally, "Make it up as you go along," a familiar American expression, appears early in the text of *Mass*.)

Mass is something of a *bricolage*—a putting together of things that are not usually thought of as belonging together as one tinkers in search of a new thing or an ingenious solution to a problem. The beginning of *Mass* mirrors the many becoming one. Seemingly unrelated vocal and instrumental lines are introduced one after the other. They pile up and jockey for position, like diversity or pluralism run amok, until the density and volume of sound reach a peak. At that point, described by Bernstein and his lyricist Stephen Schwartz as one of "maximum confusion," a single guitar chord intervenes. It silences what had sounded like senseless accumulation. And out of the brief pause that follows, the hymn "Sing God a Simple Song" rises, sung by a single voice. It begins like a simple folk song. All the other musical elements fall into place, dispelling the chaos of the opening moments.

ACTIVITY 4.6

Listen to Leonard Bernstein's Mass *in its entirety (Sony SM2K63089). Identify as many different genres (e.g., rock, ballad), types of musical ensembles (e.g., band, boys' choir), performance styles (e.g., operatic, folk), cultural influences (e.g., Latin, African) as you can find. Do they add up to or detract from the Americanness of the piece? Give the reasons for your answer.*

Mass exemplifies multiple cultural influences; Bernstein appropriated musical elements freely. Sometimes, however, composers choose to focus not only on a single culture but even more narrowly on a single but distinctive motif. George Gershwin (1898–1937) illustrates this in *Cuban Overture* (1932).

ACTIVITY 4.7

You have heard CD track 24 where the rhythm of the clave pattern is "performed" by members of the audience in a free Tito Puente concert on a New York City street. You have heard and recognized that pattern in CD track 23 where it is performed by a member of the orchestra playing Gershwin's Cuban Overture.

Try to listen to the whole of the Cuban Overture. *Despite differences in tempo, the rhythmic pattern remains the same. In each case—the first a spontaneous response from the audience at a public concert and the second, part of an art music composition written by an American for a symphony orchestra—the pattern is identifiable as Latino or Afro-Caribbean.*

Discuss the ways in which the clave pattern and the contexts of its use illustrate multiculturalism and oneness. Consider as many aspects of the musical event as you can think of (e.g., the performers, the audience—actual or intended—the composer, their respective cultural backgrounds, the medium for performance, and so on).

Gershwin wrote some of the most popular of American songs, "Oh, Lady Be Good," "Embraceable You," and "Summertime" among them. Exemplifying the fluidity of genre boundaries, his *Porgy and Bess* has been called a musical, a folk opera, or just plain opera. It has been performed on Broadway and in opera houses all over the world.

In the *Cuban Overture* Gershwin appropriates a well-known Afro-Caribbean *clave* pattern to give the composition its Cuban flavor. It is, however, only the sound that is lifted from the Afro-Caribbean context. Its function—its cultural meaning—has been altered. Whereas in Afro-Caribbean music making this pattern is what keeps all the elements, vocal and instrumental, of an ensemble together, in the Gershwin piece it is used to provide an ethnic reference, a swatch of local color. Coordinating the various parts in the performance remains in the conductor's hands.

The examples above show how musicians, singly or in small groups, have created oneness out of the diverse resources that multiculturalism and pluralism have put at their command. As *social* construction, however, the outstanding example of oneness is jazz.

Race, Oneness, and Jazz.　　Perhaps nothing exemplifies the unifying power embedded in American life as persuasively as that which produced jazz. Out of the most intense conflict and opposition between the inclusivity of America's democratic ideal and the exclusivity of racial discrimination, jazz emerged, overcoming the social stigma that had been inflicted on it and becoming America's most distinctive contribution to the world of music.

When freed slaves became members of American society, oneness had to be constructed out of one of the most divisive issues that has confronted the United States: the relations between its white and black populations. Many books have told that story. What follows is intended only to sketch the cohesive tension that opposition can generate to create unity in American musical life. The account begins with the extreme polarity with which black-white opposition began.

Early in the country's history, the framers of the American Constitution "count[ed] black slaves as three-fifths of a person" (Holmes 2001: 1). In 1858 the Dred Scott decision disqualified blacks from becoming American citizens. It is only by confronting these historical realities that we can begin to understand the great distance that needed to be traveled before integration could even be imagined. The social status of those who were to give birth to jazz was branded onto their music, and the stigma was kept fresh through almost two centuries of segregation, miscegenation laws, and a wide range of discriminatory practices that continue, albeit in attenuated forms, to the present.

The deadly nature of discrimination and one of its horrible tools—lynching—is simply but powerfully presented in "Strange Fruit" (ca. 1930) by Abel Meeropol (1903–86), a white Jewish schoolteacher who used Lewis Allan as nom de plume. Also a poet and songwriter, he is known as well as the man who took care of the children of Ethel and Julius Rosenberg after they were executed for espionage in June 1953.

"Strange Fruit" is most closely associated with Billie Holliday, one of the greatest blues singers ever, who first sang the song in 1939. "Strange Fruit" has been called a protest song, one of the first if not the first against racism. Holliday recounts that whenever she sang it in the South, there was trouble. Columbia Records, which recorded Holliday, refused to touch it.

The text is what speaks most eloquently about what people can do to those they do not consider their equal as human beings. But the music also displays differences between African American and the wider American performance practice. While using the Western European idiom and its strophic song form, the piece achieves its power through the manipulation of the melodic line. It is made to wind between and around the intended or written-down pitches in a manner left to the artistic discretion of individual performers. (So strong is the song's association with Billie Holliday, however, that few have performed it.) A number of pitches curl around single syllables of text. This is a practice commonplace in African American practice long before those features appeared in American popular music. Melody absolved from strict adherence to the rhythm and meter of its accompaniment was melody set loose to rhythmic improvisation by the principal performers.

ACTIVITY 4.8
Compare the way "Strange Fruit" (in Lady Sings the Blues, *Verve Records) is sung to Woody Guthrie's rendition of "This Land Is Your Land" (CD track 20).*

FIGURE 4.3 *Billie Holiday.* *(Photo by Carl Van Vechten. From the Library of Congress American Memory Historical Collection, Reproduction No. LC-USZ62-112865.)*

Write down the text of each song, allowing plenty of space between syllables and between lines. With an x, mark the pitch(es) you hear for each syllable.

How are the two songs similar or different:

(1) in terms of the number of pitches per syllable?
(2) in terms of the way each singer synchronizes his or her singing with the accompaniment?
(3) in any other terms that you think are significant?

The correct answers particularly to the first two questions illustrate some differences between an African American and an Anglo-American singing style.

The differences between the music that was to become jazz and the music of the American majority were much greater than musical analysis can reveal. Those differences were illumined by social relations even as these were themselves illumined by musical practice. Strict segregation rules were meant to keep the opposing groups apart. Social attitudes conditioned the perception that musically (as in other respects) black and white society were worlds apart. But these conditions could not prevent musical contact and cross-fertilization.

Thrown together outside rural contexts by the great migration that brought black musicians to major American cities like Chicago and New York after World War I, musicians from both sides of the racial divide listened to each other and interacted with increasing frequency. A trend toward cohesion was beginning to emerge, but it was met by strong opposing forces led by legally sanctioned Jim Crow practices and by the white supremacist organization the Ku Klux Klan. The conflicts, interactions, and the resulting tension were reflected in the personal experiences of musicians like the great African American trumpet player Louis Armstrong and the Anglo-American cornetist Bix Beiderbecke. They enjoyed playing together in private, one respecting and admiring the other. But despite their sterling reputation as musicians, each in his own milieu, they could not play together in public simply because one was black, the other white. Social pressures pulled them apart even as music drew them toward each other.

In 1917 jazz was recorded for the first time by an all-white band called Original Dixieland Jazz Band on claims, by its leader, that jazz was a white invention. The event indicated, among other things, that the larger American society had begun to reconsider its valuation of jazz not only as something one hears but also as social act and as commodity. On those levels, the direct and deliberate engagement of white and black America in the arena of jazz became highly visible. Whites danced to the music of black musicians even as the musicians inhabited a world different from that inhabited by the white dancers on the floor. Even at the height of Duke Ellington's fame, he could not stay at white hotels. John Hammond, a wealthy white American who had devotedly sought and supported talented jazz artists, could not find an American recording company willing to take a chance on black musicians. (A British recording company eventually did.) Although the races were integrated at the famous Savoy Ballroom in New York City's Harlem, the general rule elsewhere was segregation. Even as jazz was beginning to be broadcast nationwide and was getting introduced in concert halls, white jazz performers were being given the visible roles. The white clarinetist and bandleader Benny Goodman got the credit for filling the air time the National Broadcasting Corporation (NBC) had given to jazz even when materials and arrangements were being contributed by the black Fletcher Henderson. It was the white Benny Goodman who came to be called "the king of swing."

All these hardly begin to suggest the great complexity of the situation. But what is pertinent for this brief discussion is that despite the tortuous road, jazz managed to leave behind the segregated identity that the larger society had sought to impose upon it. Painfully at first but with increasing inevitability in the wake of social forces that finally acknowledged racism and battled against it, African American musicians finally interacted with white society—musicians and audiences—on equal terms. Interestingly, its confinement to the margins by America at large contributed to its recognition as a non-European music. This, as has been acknowledged by historians, was a necessary and major first step for American music to find an unambiguous identity that was truly its own. The music of an originally debased minority not even entitled to call itself American had become the music of the whole, a music universally recognized as quintessentially American.

The distinctiveness of jazz is broad-based. It has introduced and installed innovations in the Western European–derived pitch system of the American musical mainstream. Best known are the so-called blue notes, a marked alteration and manipulation of the third, fifth, and seventh notes of the seven-note European diatonic major scale. (Listen again to Billie Holiday and see if you can spot the blue notes.) When the pitch inventory changes, so do the melody and harmony. The twelve-bar blues form and the central role given to improvisation are decidedly African American contributions.

The use of time in music, specifically in its rhythmic organization, is jazz's outstanding and most recognizable feature. Swing has become part of the American musical vocabulary. It refers to a rhythmic feel achieved through the use of devices such as syncopation to elicit physical movement as response to the music. And jazz's organization of pitch, time, and form has created a unique musical genre that, Robert

O'Meally (Columbia University professor and founder and director of its Center for Jazz Studies) argues, is an apt metaphor for American culture as a whole (Richardson 2000: 39). Individual freedom, best expressed in the solo and the strong emphasis on improvisation, tugs and pulls at the communal spirit of ensemble work to unify opposing forces and produce a dynamic whole.

Dizzy Gillespie.   Born John Birks in 1917 in South Carolina, Dizzy Gillespie (d. 1993) went on to an illustrious career as trumpeter, bandleader, composer, ambassador of goodwill for the U.S. State Department, which sent him to perform all over the world. With little formal training, he learned the trombone, trumpet, cornet, and piano. His penchant for clowning on stage earned him the name "Dizzy." Concentrating on the trumpet and becoming a virtuoso on the instrument, Gillespie proved himself an innovator, incorporating Afro-Cuban rhythms into his compositions and helping lead the way to what came to be known as Latin jazz. In the late 1940s experiments at jam sessions with other jazz greats such as Charlie Parker, Thelonius Monk, and Kenny Clarke led to bop, a more complex version of jazz.

In "Emanon" (read it backward), the interplay of independence and dependence is notable. The solo instruments (trumpet, bass, drums, and piano in turn) seem totally free to stand out above and seemingly apart from the ensemble, to follow their creative fancy as they weave melodic lines, and to organize time uninhibited by meter and the tyranny of the bar line. But such freedom is dependent on the rock-solid stability of the rhythmic anchor provided by the ensemble.

ACTIVITY 4.9
Listen to "Emanon" (available from Laselight album Night in Tunisia, *no. 17 108, among other sources) and identify the solos, which in this piece, are extended and easy to find. But pay special attention to what the rest of the instruments are doing. Characterize and compare the rhythmic features of the solos and the ensemble.*

The opposition between solo and ensemble, between competitiveness—the individual drive to excel—and cooperation between individ-

FIGURE 4.4   *The banner of Jazz at Lincoln Center, the concert season, displayed at Avery Fisher Hall in Lincoln Center, the home of the New York Philharmonic Orchestra.   (Photo by Adelaida Reyes.)*

uals as members of a team or a community is an outstanding reflection of a larger, society-wide opposition between individualism and being part of a group. The opposition that is central to jazz resolves the dilemma of inclusiveness and exclusiveness, favoring neither but creating the kind of tension that, instead of disrupting, binds like glue. From its extremely debased position, jazz has now taken its place in conservatories and concert halls. Its elevation as American music is represented by the new jazz center that is part of New York City's and the nation's Lincoln Center. Literally and figuratively, the jazz center stands side by side with that temple of European-derived music, the Juilliard School.

THE DYNAMICS OF ONENESS

Oneness or unity is frequently associated with stability, and stability is often seen as static, or as changing at a pace so slow and gradual that

FIGURE 4.5   *Jazz at Lincoln Center, which is to house state-of-the-art facilities and a concert hall of its own, and which is to be part of the Time-Warner building, under construction in 2003 in one of the choicest locations in New York city, at Columbus Circle.   (Photo by Adelaida Reyes.)*

hardly anyone notices. How then can the fast-changing American musical scene be reconciled with cultural oneness? How do musical products as diverse as those cited in this chapter represent oneness? How can "Caverns," "Stomp Dance," and *Mass*, for example, belong to one musical lineage? What "genes" do they share?

These questions would be impossible to address if one confines oneself to sound, because musical sound as symbol or marker stands for something other than itself. It is for this reason that symbols can change even when what it stands for remains constant. Gilbert Chase has insisted that the key to American music lies in the nature of American society" (Crawford 1987: xi). That key belongs to history.

History sheds indispensable light on the events and the forces that shaped and continue to shape America, on the ideologies and values that inform American music, on the body of ideas on which American oneness rests. A firm grasp of those principles and ideas is essential because as interpreted, practiced, and enacted by the country's diverse peoples at different moments in time, they inevitably assume diverse forms. On this surface level, on the level of everyday life where music is not merely heard but lived, opposition, conflict, and competition find their arena. Here it becomes possible to observe individualism grappling with community; the spiritual with the secular; religion with crass commercialism. In this arena, diversity holds center stage. But at the deepest level abstract principles and historically sanctioned ideologies form the bedrock. Ideas such as freedom of expression, pragmatism (whatever works), ingenuity (make it up as you go along), democracy, and the idealization of the common man give the nation its common coin, instigating diversity while keeping it firmly anchored.

E pluribus unum has been called the "great national balancing act through history" (Todd 2001: 15). On one side is diversity, with its wealth of resources along with its potential for fragmentation. On the other is assimilation or uniformity, offering the comfort of predictability and generalizability while harboring the seeds both of coercion and rebellion. As in a tug of war, one side pulls against the other. Sometimes, one side seems to gain the advantage; at other times, the other side. But oneness is maintained when neither side prevails, when the opposing efforts keep the rope taut but unbroken. This is the balance that observers of the American scene, from Tocqueville in the nineteenth century to Erik Erikson, Ledeen, and Higham among others, have equated with American cohesion and oneness. It is the balance that jazz achieves between the forces that it creatively sets in opposition one to the other.

CHAPTER 5

American Musical Culture

Full of the ferment, the constant tinkering of the *bricoleur*, and the perpetual discontent that Tocqueville saw as a consequence of Americans' belief in the perfectability of things, America's musical life calls for a unifying vision. That is what this exploration has been about. While acknowledging the constantly changing surface of a life that bustles with unceasing and restless activity, the exploration has been guided by the assumption that beneath that surface are unifying forces that pull the parts into a whole that is not merely the sum of its parts. The previous chapters have proposed that in the history of what has been called the American experiment, and in a broader definition of music that does not confine itself to sound, lies the core of that unifying vision.

The incomplete pyramid on the dollar bill is a constant reminder of the nature of the task. The pyramid is a solid, stable, durable structure. But the American symbol stops short of completion. It *envisions* the finished structure; its final form to be realized in the mind of the observer or, in the case of American music, through the ear of the listener. Like Seurat's *Afternoon at la Grande Jatte*, the American pyramid requires the active participation of the observer if the image of the whole is to be constructed from those endlessly moving and changing parts. For the unifying vision, that full picture of the American musical scene, like the pyramid of the American symbol, is an ideal. Against it, the reality of bricks and mortar represented by musical sounds and human acts are measured for inclusion in the construction of the envisioned whole. That whole, in turn, is a blueprint drawn from historically validated principles of Americanness. The process-orientedness of this ongoing bridge building between reality and vision characterizes American musical culture.

A VIEW THROUGH TECHNOLOGY

A look at today's musical scene from the perspective of technology and its impact on American musical life affords a glimpse of the ways in which this orientation toward process is manifested. The speed with which technology innovates and induces innovation in fields such as music makes it possible to observe over a relatively short time processes that have previously taken more than a lifetime. Technology seems to compress time—between an idea and its realization, between the introduction of something new and its social acceptance or rejection. And while the barrage of new things that technology foists upon us seems to tip the balance heavily in diversity's favor, the forces that make some of the new things persist and others fade away compel us to look beyond the here and now. To legitimize its claim to Americanness, the contemporary reaches back to the historical. At the same time, the historical counts on the contemporary for its perpetuation.

Technology and Contemporary Frontier Pushing.   At the time of the nation's birth and decades past its infancy, American growth was fueled by a drive to push geographic boundaries. As the population grew and spread over the land, frontiers shrank, and in time they became more metaphorical than actual. Frontier pushing moved to the realm of ideas, to be translated back and given concrete form by American pragmatism. Over the years, testing limits became ingrained into the American character. To Geoffrey O'Brien, an Americanist and editor-in-chief of the Library of America, the "whole point [of American culture] is to find out what happens when every form of restriction is removed" (1999: 42).

O'Brien's observation resonates in American musical life. Challenging musical boundaries is the musical equivalent of frontier pushing, and in contemporary America, nothing exemplifies it more dramatically than music supported by technology. Together, music and technology push musical boundaries or leap across them to create new ones. Yet even as they seem intent on making the past irrelevant, they awaken old concerns. Sound resources and their manipulation to create music, the production and dissemination of music, the qualifications of those who would be called musicians, music as property and the ethics governing its use: these are some age-old issues that keep reappearing, transposed to a new key. They are the past establishing their continuity with the present and reclaiming their place in it.

At the Frontier of Musical Sound.   The intermittently recurring question of what sounds are musical and what are not has been made inevitable by technology and its seemingly unlimited capacity for creating sounds that may or may not be admissible to existing musical systems. These new sounds seduce creative artists to challenge the boundaries of those systems and to find ways to let the new sounds in. The tension between sounds that already have a function in the system and are thus considered musical and those sounds that seek to alter the system so that they can find a function within it blurs the line that separates the musical from the nonmusical. The result is the expansion of the world of musical sound and the creation of new contexts for its use. The contemporary acoustic landscape has become a kaleidoscope of new pitches, tone colors, and textures out of which new ideas and new forms of musical expression emerge.

ACTIVITY 5.1

Select one piece of music that you consider a good example of an expansion of sound resources beyond those offered by acoustic instruments. Write an essay about your selection that addresses the following:

- The nature of the "expansion" that you hear.
- The use of technology by artists.
- The context: Who are the musicians? What is the music intended for?

Wherever technology is used in the service of sound, the above observations are likely to apply. But the specifics—the boundaries in contention, their creative resetting, the resulting forms, and the speed with which new forms emerge, for instance—contain the markers that can point to things identifiably American.

Genre and Other Boundaries. The increasing frequency with which terms like *crossover*, *hybrid*, and *fusion* are being used suggests a growing fluidity if not a downright breaching of boundaries that define genres and make them distinguishable.

ACTIVITY 5.2

Bring to class a sample of what you consider to be rock music. Be prepared to articulate in class why you consider it rock and what its defining features are. In class discussion, compare your definition and selection with those of your classmates. The point is to consider what your observations say about the nature of the boundaries that define rock as a genre. Are those boundaries firm? fluid? irrelevant?

The constant challenge to boundaries, however, does not signal destruction or deterioration. Rather, the challenge often gives rise to at least one response to the question that Geoffrey O'Brien has placed at the center of American culture: What happens when restrictions—such as those imposed by genre boundaries—are removed? New growths appear. Prodded by technology in combination with pluralism and its effects on musical resources, by individualism, and by the American preference for innovation over conservation, testing the limits and pushing the envelope not only make new growths inevitable but also gives the resulting forms an American cast.

Rap (the musical concept as distinct from an African American style of talk), for example, came out of the practice of DJs who periodically interjected spoken text into the music they spun. Using two turntables and a mixer, they coaxed new sounds out of prerecorded music on vinyl discs. As spinning itself evolved into an art—one that involved a growing number of mechanical paraphernalia and demanded the full attention of the instrumentalist—DJs hired MCs who could rhyme (Keyes 2002). Meanwhile, African American speech that was street-savvy and urban had come into its own as a form of literary expression. These two facets of what started out as a street activity in the Bronx (New York City), one belonging squarely to the realm of speech, the other to that of music, seemed initially to keep their autonomy. They were going hand in hand, moving in the same direction, but each kept to its side of the speech-music divide. Eventually, however, the literary and the musical pushed against the boundaries that kept them apart. They found a common function and brought a new genre into existence. Rap evolved into a distinctively American form, born of a speech-music union on American streets, aided and abetted by American urban social conditions, and infused with stunning speed into the national consciousness by technology and the media.

Similarly, the new fluidity of the lines separating the aural from the visual in the arts has given rise to new synergies. Dancers' movements have been converted into sound by sensors attached to the dancers' bodies. Activated by movement, the sensors transmit the signals that become the music to which the dancers dance. "Pikapika," for example, is a collaborative solo performance character created by Tomie Hahn, a dancer, and composer Curtis Bahn. The piece is an interactive composition employing a custom-made wearable dance interface. As Hahn's costume sends information about her movements to an offstage computer, actions are converted to sound which are transmitted back to small speakers mounted on her body. (The collaboration is described more fully in Hahn and Bahn 2003.)

Russell Pinkston's "Song for the Living/Dance for the Dead" (2000) calls for a MIDI touch-sensitive dance floor. This allows the movement of dancers to send signals and to software that then processes those signals for real-time sound and video creation.

Alvin Lucier's "I Am Sitting in a Room" exemplifies what has been called "sound art." The piece tweaks the line that separates musical from nonmusical sound and in the process challenges as well the traditional concept of musician and musical instrument The composer recites over and over again a text that describes what he is doing. "I am . . . recording the sound of my speaking voice and I am going to play it back into the room again and again . . . until the resonant frequencies of the room reinforce themselves so that any semblance of my speech, with perhaps the exception of rhythm, is destroyed. What you will hear, then, are the natural resonant frequencies of the room articulated by speech." The article from which this passage is quoted is tellingly titled "It's Sound, It's Art, and Some Call It Music." The composer, teacher, and writer Kyle Gann, who wrote the article, suggests that the room in which the reading took place is a musical instrument. The room, made resonant by the composer's voice, which itself was transformed as the room resonated, created the sounds out of which the piece was constructed. The performance was billed as an exhibit that affords a look at "music from the visual-art point of view" (2000: 41).

Laurie Anderson, an artist who uses images as readily as she does sounds, is sometimes classified as a visual artist and placed alongside other visual artists such as Jasper Johns, Robert Rauschenberg, and Andy Warhol. But she is also claimed by art and popular music. She creates large-scale multimedia works with titles like *Moby Dick* and *United States I–IV*, invents instruments like the "talking stick," which can digitally process a wide range of sounds, and uses visual cues such as the American flag and the dollar sign.

In creating a sound art category and making it eligible for grants, the Guggenheim Foundation, whose fellowship awards to scholars and

FIGURE 5.1 *Tomie Hahn performing "Pikspika"* *(Photo courtesy of Tomie Hahn and Curtis Bahn.)*

artists in all fields are among the most prestigious in the nation, has signaled the passage of "sound art" from individual innovation to social institutionalization.

In an environment where sequences of sound can be technologically rearranged or recombined, the limits and constraints that genres and systems in general can impose on musical structure are easily undermined. With the definition of musical sound under extreme pressure, with the production of sound used for musical purposes no longer consigned to musical instruments alone, with the impact of these on musical genres, styles, and forms in general, it was only a matter of time before the label *musician* also came up for re-examination.

Who Is a Musician? When the technologically lowly turntable became a musical instrument to be manipulated and persuaded to yield new sounds by people with imagination, good memory, quick reflexes, and manual dexterity, those who did the manipulating came to be known first as DJs, then as "turntablists." Calling them musicians has met with resistance, but voices arguing the turntablists' case on the grounds that they produce essentially new compositions are growing in number. Mim Udovitch, a contributing editor at the magazine *Rolling Stone*, contends that the DJ's product is a species of electronic composition (2000: 11). Kai Fikentscher, in his book *"You Better Work": Underground Dance Music in New York* (2000), argues that the product of "turntabling" or "spinning" is vernacular art.

Fikentscher provides the following description of CD tracks 33a and 33b:

> Ali N. Askin's "Mart" (CD track 33a), which forms the basis for Fikentscher's remix, "Mart(-inique)" (CD track 33b), is an ambient electronic music piece based on a combination of a vocal sample extracted from a recording of Morton Feldman's "Three Voices," and a sample from a recording of "Magic," a composition by drummer Billy Cobham. Using a vocoder (a synthesizer that, when used on samples of the human voice, makes the voice sound disembodied), the Feldman sample was substantially altered, using the rhythmic structure of the Cobham sample. To thicken the texture, Askin added many more samples, including those of static noise from various vinyl recordings; snippets (mainly vocal) of several classical rhythm and blues and film soundtrack recordings; and a portion of one of his own piano compositions which was recorded backwards for inclusion in "Mart" (not heard in CD track 34a but heard in 34b). The electronic treatment of the component sounds makes each inextricable from the others; none is traceable to its original source. "Mart" is a copyrighted piece of original music.
>
> Fikentscher's remix aims at making "Mart" more danceable and engaging. To this end, and as a first step toward the creation of "Mart (-inique)," "Mart" is speeded up from 119 bpm (beats per minute) to 123. Dispensing with sequencing software, Fikentscher adds to the original structure two percussion loops and two trumpet motifs, all taken from commercial vinyl recordings of late twentieth-century rhythm and blues. Finally, flanging and echo effects are added at various points to heighten the musical "drama." (Flanging is a type of "inaudible" delay effect which is heard as a swooping sound. In "Mart(-inique)" such an effect is heard especially after the reverse Askin piano excerpt which serves as a bridge to return to the main theme.) (Personal communication.)

Different versions of "Mart(-inique)" are being created as this work in progress evolves. But the extremely abbreviated sketch given here bolsters Fikentscher's contention that remixes such as "Mart(-inique)" are instances of contemporary DJ practice that make a legitimate claim to being both original compositions as well as original performances.

FIGURE 5.2   *Kai Fikentscher, ethnomusicologist and DJ/turntablist, working with mixer and turntable.*   *(Photo by Muema Lombe. Used with permission.)*

The ambiguity of attitudes toward the product rubs off on the way their practitioners are identified. Rap performers, whose art straddles the boundaries of speech and music, are referred to as rappers, rap artists, and rap stars, seldom if ever as singers or musicians. Gil Scott-Herron, an important influence on rap, has been called a poet-musician whose works are referred to as song poems, but he denies being a poet, composer, or musician (Keyes 2002: 35).

Similarly, the ambiguous status in the field of music of those whose work is generated or aided by technology may be reflected in their work. Without the skills attained in formal music training (e.g., reading conventional music notation) but highly adept at electronic devices such as computers, turntables, mixers, and samplers, their work often raises the question, Is it music?

The Production and Dissemination of Music. Without the relatively simple technologies of overdubbing and multitracking, we would never have heard Natalie Cole singing duets with her dead father, Nat "King" Cole. Without the relatively sophisticated techniques of sampling, the seamless patching together of musical fragments from a variety of sources, written by a variety of composers, and realized by a variety of performers who may or may not be called musicians could never have amounted to a piece of music. Tape loops, which go around and around repeating musical segments, have become a convenience to minimalists, who believe in the expressive power of repetition. From the composers Philip Glass and Steve Reich to rappers on streets and subway stations equipped with drum machines, tape players, and other sound paraphernalia, repetitiveness as a musical device has claimed its share of the contemporary musical scene, thanks in no small part to the endless mechanical repetition made possible by technology.

That artists can now work directly with sound without needing to master the musical vocabulary and the grammatical and syntactic rules of a conventional musical language has facilitated musical interaction among those who come from different musical cultures and use different musical languages. The skill of reading a music score and imagining what it sounds like is going the way of the handwritten letter and its evocation of the writer's voice. Many performers and conductors are no longer content to sit down with a score, conjuring its realization in sound. With increasing frequency, they ask composers to provide computer playback along with the score. Similarly, publishers expect composers to produce scores at home using a computer and printer.

With the cat-and-mouse game being played by computer programmers and Internet companies on the one hand, and record companies on the other (to be discussed in more detail below), musicians are gaining new insights into ways of profiting more directly from their work. They license their creations to advertising companies and to film, television, and radio. Musicians and composers, particularly those who are not yet widely known, get the advantage of broad exposure and a quicker return on their creative investment. They bypass the expensive manufacturing, distribution, and promotion services that record companies use to market their musical products. In this way, the artists eliminate the need to wait for royalties that depend on the sale of records.

Technology and the media have had an enormous impact on the dissemination of music. Ever faster computers, broad-band transmission and other devices for duplication and communication, the improvement of sound reproduction, and the various enhancements to musical connectivity have involved more people in musical life than ever before. Economics, law, and ethics are playing larger roles in the field of music.

Music as Property and as Commodity. Debates are ongoing about the fairness of lifting a sound from someone else's composition—say, something as short as a cymbal crash or a musical motif—and dropping it into one's own without permission from its source. When the writer Tony Scherman noted that such appropriation is acceptable as a part of music making (1999: 49), no one hoisted a red flag. A few years ago, he would have sparked a lively if not heated debate on the ethical and aesthetic issues that such a statement raises. Scherman underscores the change in values assigned to borrowing, appropriating, or lifting that has already taken hold: Made easy and commonplace by technology, those practices, Scherman contends, are like "creative rummaging [which has become] the crucial talent, supplanting the traditional virtues of imagination and technique" (ibid.).

The legality of certain practices involving the copying and distribution of music has raised the music-as-commodity view to new heights and has made ever more visible the huge overlap between music and money in American musical culture. Music is property that has a price tag and can be stolen. A few years ago and before recording companies and the courts intervened, the Internet companies Napster and MP3 made it possible to download an extraordinary range of music through websites. These technologies promoted the dissemination of music for free. But in the process, it is claimed, users of these technologies deprive composers and songwriters of revenues in the form of royalties. Most important to America's corporate world, they cut into the profits of record companies.

The legal eruptions that followed the filing of lawsuits by the Recording Industry Association of America, first against Napster and subsequently against downloaders and file sharers in general, rumbles on ominously. Giant record companies continue to threaten legal action to protect their interests from what they see as piracy and trafficking in stolen goods. Programmers and companies meanwhile keep looking for new ways to bypass the restrictions being imposed and to keep downloading and sharing music files as cost-free to consumers as possible. Online service providers and net sites refuse to be intimidated. Kazaa, RealOne Rhapsody, MusicNet, MusicMatch, Grokster, BearShare, AOL MusicNet, eMusic, and iTunes are only some of the entries into the field of music downloading. More will surely appear. All are attracted by the great money-making potential of the music download business. The stakes are high. Sanford C. Bernstein & Company, a research firm in New

York, had "predicted that 16% or $985 million of the nation's music sales in 2002 would be lost to what it termed Web piracy" (Foege 2000: 4).

That music is a commodity that can be bought and sold is underscored by the attention paid to numbers. There is no shortage of agencies (such as SoundScan and comScore Media Metrix) and publications (such as *Billboard*) that compile statistics on how many records are bought and sold and in what categories. Marketing executives for record companies keep their eyes on "the charts" that track those statistics.

There is no shortage of things to count either: concert attendance, the price of artists' contracts, the cost of tickets and subscriptions, the budgets for productions, the revenues they bring in, and so on. These may not be heard directly in the music, but they underpin what we hear and can well dictate what we don't hear in certain venues. What the CD that accompanies this book contains, for example, depended only in part on the author's choice. What could be included was substantially affected by permissions granted or denied, or by the prohibitive costs being charged by record companies that owned the rights.

It is thus not without reason that a constellation of activities that have to do with creating, producing, and disseminating music has come to be labeled the music *industry*. It is not surprising that one of the most authoritative measures of success in the industry is quantitative: the number of records sold and the widely advertised awards that underscore that success. The bling-bling mentality, a term that originated with rappers and hip-hoppers, refers to the creation and performance of music with an eye to material returns. And the efficacy with which statistics are compiled and used has been greatly enhanced and encouraged by technological means now easily accessible for use in the promotion, sale, and distribution of music.

Applause meters, sales figures, and the number of music consumers of course do not constitute an aesthetic judgment. Their significance lies in the habits of heart—those parts of a culture's DNA—that frequency of occurrence and widespread use reflect. In a market-oriented culture like that of the United States, for instance, they demonstrate what Tocqueville saw wherever he went in the country: the "intense love of wealth" (1856: 19), its pursuit, and their offspring—the entrepreneurial ethos. These values are threaded through American history and are very much in evidence in today's America.

BEYOND TECHNOLOGY: THE LARGER PICTURE

In the mid-twentieth century, electronic music—music that is electronically generated or altered—was new, esoteric, and by today's standards, quite primitive. It was created by a small group of highly trained musicians and composers working in laboratories with prohibitively expensive equipment that took up a lot of room. The work often involved more than one composer: Otto Luening and Vladimir Ussachevsky, Milton Babbit and Mario Davidovsky were among the best-known pairs.

Changes in the acoustic aspects of music quickly revealed the awkwardness of the fit between sound and context. In concert halls, the primary function of which was to showcase live performers, electronic music seemed alien. Audiences faced an empty stage equipped with speakers from which sounds emanated. The disconnect shook norms of behavior. Not infrequently, someone would whisper after all the sounds had died down, "Do we clap?" Unless the composers were present, there was no one to take bows and acknowledge applause.

Today, sound and context have come closer together in venues that better suit electronically- or computer-generated music when seeing a live performer working on synthesizers, mixers, and other such equipment adds little to the experience of listening. Such music is now more likely to be heard in spaces where people can walk around, dance, or stay still if they wish, but need no longer remain seated in rows facing a seemingly abandoned stage. The entire configuration of music as an organism that consists not only of sound but of human behavior within a given space and under particular circumstances has been altered. The alteration has been both cause and effect of changes in the sounds of music and the means and motivation for their production.

As a consequence of these developments, the very term *electronic music* now smacks of obsolescence, and there is as yet no institutionally sanctioned term that embraces the musical field that technology has created. Socially, in a process that can be called democratization, the old exclusivity—a consequence of the highly specialized training required of those who would create it and those who would be its consumers—has given way to inclusivity. Lower production costs, more efficient machines that can be operated with a modicum of technical training, and networks that reach a wider circle of prospective users have all made themselves felt. By the end of the twentieth century, a single individual, with or without formal musical training, can sit alone in a small room with a computer, a sampler, and relevant software to create music. The partnership between music and technology has become ubiquitous on all levels of American society. It has invaded clubs and has been happily adopted by rappers on the street, hip-hoppers, dancers, high- and low-budget movies, advertisers, and sound artists who work directly with sound for immediate or future use.

That partnership and the changes they have wrought provide an excellent demonstration of a process that subsumes those that have been described so far: the process of finding coherence in what appears to be a sea of innovations. The linguist Michael Shapiro's observations pertaining to language recommend themselves to music. "Innovations," he wrote, "are produced by individuals, whereas change is social fact" (1991: 8–9). The potential for chaos that American individualism can impose on the musical scene—a chaos that Gell-Mann sees as essential in complex societies (see the last section of chapter 2)—is made orderly by society's actions upon them. But such order is never final. In American society, the dynamics are ongoing, history-driven, and part of American self-definition. Individuals can be counted on to push the limits that order and the need for stability impose.

Thus opposition is kept alive, and the balance and cohesive tension that undergirds American oneness is maintained. As the new proliferates, the old and the traditional reassert their claims. New and old compete, coexist, cooperate. Laptops, oscillators, samplers, microchips, and a host of sound-producing and sound-altering gadgets displace old sounds and at the same time conserve and enhance them. Hip-hop, electronica, garage, and other types of music considered current not only coexist with but appropriate music of earlier vintages—the golden oldies, items from the American songbook (the repertory of popular song classics), items from the classical repertoire. Industry encourages innovation; institutions and government sponsor symphony orchestras and opera houses. Singers with body mikes thrive alongside singers with formidable techniques that can project the voice to the last row of the largest concert halls. Banjos and acoustic guitars coexist with their amplified counterparts. Old instruments hold their value, and their sounds find new roles in the most contemporary musical compositions. Jazz continues to evolve, and folk forms like the square dance and the polka continue to enliven the musical scene. The tug of war between diversity and oneness gives American musical life its particular vibrancy.

The picture has not and promises not to become simpler, but the underlying principles, though subject to interpretation and reinterpretation, remain constant. Thus Kyle Gann, convinced that generalizing from the diversity of sounds will not work, echoes what Gilbert Chase has been advocating since the middle of the twentieth century. Instead of searching for Americanness in "the qualities of the music itself," Gann argues, it would be "more fruitful . . . to look for the nature of American music in the social conditions that all American composers share"

(1997: xiv). Gann's subject matter is American art music or, as he prefers to call it, classical music; hence his focus on composers. But his argument is valid on a larger scale. There is now abundant evidence that, at least at this point in America's young life, history and social context provide better clues to a unifying vision than sound alone can.

A SHIFT IN PERSPECTIVE

Perhaps, then, we need to be asking a different question. "What is American music?" or "What is America's music?" carries the baggage of primarily sound-oriented studies and definitions of music. Asking instead "What about a given music is American?" shifts the burden onto the historical, the social, and the cultural, where identification, for reasons given particularly in chapter 4, finds more solid ground.

The composition 4'33" (1952) by John Cage (1912–92) serves to illustrate the potential merits of this approach. The piece is a highly atypical example, but it is precisely what makes it atypical, namely, the absence of prescribed sounds, that dramatizes the usefulness of reframing the question we ask of America's music.

In the best-known performance of 4'33", the pianist David Tudor went onstage with a stopwatch in his hand. He lifted the piano lid and clicked on the stopwatch to indicate that the piece had begun. Closing and reopening the piano lid three times, Tudor suggested a three-movement structure. Otherwise, he sat quietly. At the end of four minutes and thirty-three seconds, Mr. Tudor shut the piano lid for the last time and walked off the stage.

Dubbed a "silent piece" or "Silent Sonata" or, more recently, an essay on silence (see Crawford 2001: 708; Yates 1967: 11, 325; Kozinn 2002)—"silent" because it offers no sound, and "sonata" because of its implied three-movement structure—the piece provoked a loud outcry from the press. Some critics called it an outrage, a scandal. Others called it a work of genius. It sparked many lively debates. But unlike most debates about the merits—or lack thereof—of a performance, those provoked by the "Silent Sonata" could not take on the sounds because none were in evidence. The debates raged instead around a host of other issues, musical and social, that anticipated those that are being raised today. What distinguishes musical sound from noise? What is the nature of musical composition? What are the roles of the composer, the performer, and the audience in the creation, realization, and reception of the work?

Cage himself answered some of these questions. Within a time frame of four minutes and thirty-three seconds, which he provided, the boundaries that separated composer, performer, and audience were to be dismantled as all became participants in the creation of a piece of music. What the work required of each participant was conscious and intent listening to the sounds around them. It required an awakened imagination that would make of these sounds whatever the participants wished. The silence that concertgoers think of as the absence of musical sound was to be rethought as the silence in which sounds invariably occur. For as Cage discovered when he entered a chamber from which the most advanced technology of his time had presumably removed all sound, there remained the sounds produced by Cage's own body. Sounds plucked from what surrounds the participants are therefore to be what found objects are to visual artists—materials out of which to create, with the outcome shaped both by the available materials and by each person's taste and creative ability.

Those who went along with Cage's ideas reported an intense listening experience and a renewed awareness and appreciation of sounds in the environment that they would otherwise have filtered out. They reported a feeling of inclusion in the collective work of those participating in the performance even if they knew that each participant would come up with a different product. Those who insisted, however, that composers, performers, and audiences have different and mutually exclusive roles felt frustrated if not defrauded.

In a performance I once attended in an auditorium in Los Angeles, I was impressed by the silence—deeper, it seemed, than that which descended on an audience when a conventional performance was about to start. The audience knew what they were going to be expected to do and were waiting to respond. When the piece began, the seeming motionlessness of those in attendance was punctuated at one point by a woman who stood up. She walked to a dark corner of the hall and quietly danced as though to something she was hearing with her inner ear. On another occasion, the "performer" was a man with a guitar, who picked it up as though to play it, and set it down to suggest "movements" in the piece. More recently, in April 2002, it was presented by the Eos Orchestra under the direction of Tan Dun.

What is American about this work?

John Cage was born and educated in the United States, where he resided all his life. He studied with well-known and highly respected American (Henry Cowell, for example) and European teachers (e.g., Arnold Schoenberg, a Viennese composer and the architect of twelve-tone composition). But like the cultural sponge to which American cul-

FIGURE 5.3   *"Messages" by Corinne Borgnet. The installation, consisting of a species of found objects—used Post-it notes of all sizes and colors—arranged on a fourteen-foot styrofoam tower, was exhibited at Buell Hall, Columbia University, in New York City in 2002. The used Post-its, sent to the artist in response to a notice she had posted on a storefront window, contained messages such as "Tom, your shrink called." Borgnet, who studied at l'Ecole des Beaux-Arts in Paris, encouraged viewers to stick their own Post-its to the styrofoam tower to simulate the Tower of Babel. The Post-its, each with its message, might convey either the visual equivalent of a cacophony of voices, or the viewer's own narratives constructed from the posted messages.* (Photo by Adelaida Reyes.)

ture has been compared, he had also soaked up influences from Indian and Indonesian music as well as from Oriental philosophy. According to his friend Peter Yates, a music critic and author, Zen Buddhism "liberated him [John Cage] from many of our habitual fallacies, at once reverent and comedic; [Cage's art] expects that one will receive the unexpected with an undifferentiated attention and enjoy . . . whatever one discovers" (1967: 11). (This expectation can be brought to bear on interpreting both 4'33" as well as Borgnet's *Messages*.) Innovation is written all over his work. Cage's musical frontier pushing eventually came to profoundly influence the way people make, hear, and think about music, art or popular. And like many of his modern counterparts, he was described ambiguously as a philosopher and inventor as well as a composer.

4'33" reflects the ideological underpinnings and the process-orientedness of America's music. In the allotted time, which serves as frame for the canvas that is the silence conventionally understood, the egalitarian principle admits the participation of anyone regardless of training, cultural background, or musical predilections. This inclusivity extends to the sounds that are to be the raw materials for the piece. All sounds that occur during the designated period qualify.

Raphael Mostel, a composer and a friend of Cage's, believes that "a very American sense of freedom" permeates Cage's work and may account for what musicians everywhere refer to as his liberating influence (2002: AR31). In 4'33" freedom of choice is exercised by all participants: each can treat whatever materials he or she chooses, unrestricted by established musical systems and their hierarchies. The individual is in command of all facets of the work, from its inception to its final design to the manner of its performance. Each realization, each performance of the piece is a testament to diversity, requiring a fresh conceptualization and a fresh set of construction procedures to be imposed on a fresh set of sounds.

At the same time, limits are set, and all who participate must submit to the conditions that the composer has imposed. They must adhere to the time frame, without which the piece does not exist. Within the frame participants must listen, imagine, create, or else they will leave blank the canvas—the silence—that has been laid out for them. These are the "rules of the game," the organizing principle, the wellspring of order that prevents creative freedom from degenerating into chaos.

ACTIVITY 5.3

Perform Cage's 4'33" in the company of others if possible. At the end of four minutes and thirty-three seconds, compare expe-

riences—what each one heard, what each one chose to use, what each one came up with, and how each one felt about the experience.

Did the fact that you could use whatever sounds were around you during the four minutes and thirty-three seconds make you feel free? Did it make you feel constrained? What do you think made you feel free? Constrained?

Did this experience give you any insights into the nature of freedom—of choice, of expression? Is it a privilege? Is it a burden? Put the discussion within the framework of American ideology—of what Americans and non-Americans understand as freedom.

4'33" compels the participant to assume the triple role of co-composer, performer, and listener, each equal in importance to the other. Consciously or not, the participant must then confront and resolve in his or her own way issues in opposition: freedom and constraint; randomness, diversity, and their organization into a unified whole; innovation and convention. Though implicit in all creative work, these oppositions are presented in *4'33"* under an unusual set of circumstances that make them specific to the work. They must be dealt with simultaneously by the co-composer, performer, and listener, and they must find resolution almost instantaneously within the given time frame.

Forty years ago, it became part of ethnomusicology's canon that music is not merely sound. More than sound, it is the context (social, cultural, and historical) out of which cultural meaning emerges, the means of producing sound, the concepts and behaviors behind such production. All of these are essential parts of the whole that is called music. Often, it is not only permissible but even desirable to isolate a part for the sake of better understanding the constellation to which it belongs. The analysis of sound, for example, is indispensable for understanding the internal logic and the internal structure of a composition—how it is built, how the parts hold together, how the composition is coherent. But questions of meaning and questions of identity—of Americanness— require more of sound than its integrity as a composition or as a repertory. They require that sound, having been isolated in order to be better understood as acoustic component, be put back in the service of the larger whole to which it belongs. Hence the need for history, ideology, and social context.

That is an important lesson that 4'33" compels us to confront. By omitting prescribed sound, it holds in abeyance the impulse to draw the lines around sound and to focus exclusively on it. Instead, it directs the attention first to the larger universe to which sound belongs. This shift in perspective—from the whole to its parts, rather than the other way round; from the Americanness of a culture to the Americanness of the music it labels—puts us in a better position to watch musical identity in the making.

WE, THE PEOPLE

"We, the *people* of the United States . . . do ordain and establish this Constitution" is the first sentence of that remarkable document's Preamble (emphasis added). American presidents address the country's citizens as "fellow Americans." The emphasis is on a people to whom has been vested power in a manner no other nation has done before. Americans as "common people" define themselves by their disavowal of governance by a royalty or a privileged class. Their commonness lies in values and beliefs held in common, from the president to the last citizen, upon which rests their power to govern and "to ordain" their nation's Constitution. These are the people whose musical life is the stuff of American musical culture.

For much too long, studies of music, particularly those that use the great-men, great-works approach, have ignored or neglected that part of the musical picture that is inhabited by listeners, the music users. This neglect is inexcusable when the subject is musical culture. It is especially so when the culture in question prides itself on the primacy it gives to the sovereignty of the people. It is therefore fitting that this exploration ends by casting the spotlight on those without whom there is no musical culture.

The term *popular* has the same root as *people* (Latin: *popolo, popolare*). The commonness of popular music has the same source as the commonness of the common people—the breadth of its distribution and its common use suggest general comprehensibility and widely held norms and values. The critic and writer Gerald Marzorati calls attention to popular music's many functions, some more recently developed than others. Popular music, he notes, is "a tool in the construction of individual identity." It is an effective medium for communication among different social and cultural groups. It is a "catalyst for social change, and . . . a symbol of 'America' to both ourselves and the world" (1999: 180). Marzorati makes clear that he is not attributing these functions to popular music's "styles" and sounds. These he considers ephemeral; they belong to the passing scene. What he is referring to are the growing social functions of the music in whatever generic or stylistic guise it comes. Adding his voice to those of Gilbert Chase and Kyle Gann, Marzorati finds that the significance of popular music emerges out of its common use by the common people in the activities of daily life. In this sense, popular music is the *vox populi*, the voice of the people. Jon Pareles, a *New York Times* critic, translates the popular sentiment into the language of power. The listeners, he believes, will be the final arbiters of what in music is worth saving (2000: 86).

The specifically American character of popular music's preeminent place in the nation's culture is suggested by the way America's music has been identified abroad: for more than a hundred years, it has been identified with jazz and popular music. That identification is underscored through comparison. "When Tschaikovsky died," the American composer John Adams observed, "they closed the schools in Leningrad. When Verdi died it was a day of national mourning in Italy. Today only the death of someone like John Lennon can cause that kind of national trauma" (quoted in *Newsweek* 1999:84).

In the American context, the historically validated power of popular music is demonstrated statistically by measures that are themselves reflections of the nation's values. The collective ear of the nation's people who make music popular through common use is the musical analogue of Seurat's and pointillism's viewer's eye. That ear is what must draw together the myriad islands of sound that American diversity provides so that an aural image of a unified whole can be envisioned. For no matter what sophisticated criteria are eventually developed for recognizing American musical culture, the ultimate measure is whether it can be recognized as such by the nation's people.

This is the heart of the enterprise. Everyday life has a fast turnover. History takes the long view. A partnership of the two reveals the sense of order, unity, and coherence that, over time, makes its sounds identifiable as part of a musical culture and, to the collective ear, as its own.

ENDNOTE

The Founding Fathers planted a seed, an idea wrapped in the words "E pluribus unum," in soil prepared by the Declaration of Independence and all the events surrounding its creation. What grew out of that seed was a deeply rooted tree, a system sturdy enough to withstand its powerful internal drives and to sustain the myriad graftings of immigrant cultures. It is an emergent organism, one that "is determined not by the character of its elements but by a certain organizing principle which makes these elements into a unity and imparts to them a special significance" (Greenfeld 1992: 7). What grows aboveground changes with the cultural seasons and with the new infusions that it sustains. Those growths are musical life's external forms and attributes. What anchors and sustains that huge, complex, ever changing structure grows downward, deep into the earth, practically invisible yet undoubtedly there, because how else can the visible display stand?

Neither what rises aboveground nor what digs deep into the soil tells the story of music in America. One, cut off from the other, languishes and dies. Only the conjoining of the two—of the kaleidoscopic exterior and its hidden source of energy, of sound and the forces that shape it, of the contemporary and the historical—can take on the challenge that is the question, What about this music is American?

References

Abbreviations:
New York Times: NYT
New York Review of Books: NYRB

Barth, Fredrik. 1969. Introduction. In *Ethnic Groups and Boundaries: The Social Organization of Difference,* ed. Fredrik Barth, 9–38. Boston: Little, Brown.

Barton, Josef. 2001. Preface to "Integrating America. The Problem of Assimilation at the Turn of the Century" in Higham 2001, p. 84.

Bernstein, Leonard, and Stephen Schwartz. 1971. *Leonard Bernstein's Mass* (notes to the original recording). New York: G. Schirmer.

Burkhead, Paul. 1994. "Stirring the Pot: Immigrant and Refugee Challenges to the United States and the World." In *Refugees and International Population Flows,* vol. 47, no. 2 of *Journal of International Affairs.* 579–88. New York: Columbia University.

Burns, Ken. 2001. *Jazz* (a 10-episode film for television first shown on the Public Broadcasting System in 2001).

Chase, Gilbert. 1987 [1966, 1955]. *America's Music: From the Pilgrims to the Present.* Urbana: University of Illinois Press.

Copland, Aaron. 1959. *Music and the Imagination: The Charles Eliot Norton Lectures, 1951–1952.* New York: Mentor Books.

Crawford, Richard. 2001. *America's Musical Life: A History.* New York: Norton.

———. 1993. *The American Musical Landscape.* Berkeley and Los Angles: University of California Press.

———. 1987. Foreword. In H. Wiley Hitchcock, *America's Music,* 3d ed., xi–xxiv. Urbana: University of Illinois Press.

Erikson. Erik H. 1974. *Dimensions of a New Identity: The 1973 Jefferson Lectures in the Humanities.* New York: Norton.

Ferris, Timothy. 1995. "On the Edge of Chaos." *NYRB* (September 21), 40–43.

Fikentscher, Kai. 2000. *"You Better Work": Underground Dance Music in New York City.* Hanover, N.H.: Wesleyan University Press.

Foege, Alec. 2001. "Record Labels Are Hearing an Angry Song." *NYT* (June 11), B4.

Foner, Eric. 1998. *The Story of American Freedom.* New York: Norton.

Frederickson, George M. 2002. "Wise Man." *NYRB* (February 28), 37–39.

Fricke, David. 1999. "Songs for Woodstock." Liner notes for *Jimi Hendrix Live at Woodstock*, MCAD2-11987.

Gann, Kyle. 1997. *American Music in the Twentieth Century.* New York: Schirmer Books.

———. 2000. "It's Sound, It's Art, and Some Call It Music." *NYT* (January 9), AR41–42.

Gleason, Philip.1980. "American Identity and Americanization." In *The Harvard Encyclopedia of American Ethnic Groups*, edited by Stephan Thernstrom et al., 31–58. Cambridge, Mass.: Harvard University Press.

Greenfeld, Liah. 1992. *Nationalism: Five Roads to Modernity.* Cambridge, Mass.: Harvard University Press.

Griffiths, Paul. 2001. "American Music That Rattled Berlin." *NYT* (January 14), 35, 40.

Hahn, Tomie and Curtis Bahn. 2003. "Pikapika—The Collaborative Composition of an Interactive Sonic Character" in *Organized Sound: An International Journey of Music Technology*, vol. 7, no. 3.

Higham, John. 2001. *Hanging Together: Unity and Diversity in American Culture.* Edited by Carl J. Guarneri. New Haven, Conn.: Yale University Press.

Holmes, Steven A. 2001. "The Confusion over Who We Are." *NYT* (June 3), 1, 5.

Holt, Elizabeth Gilmore.1966. *From the Classicists to the Impressionists: A Documentary History of Art and Architecture in the Nineteenth Century.* New York: Anchor Books.

Kennedy, David M. 2002. "The Party's Still Not Over." *NYT* (March 3), WK3.

Keyes, Cheryl. 2002. *Rap Music and Street Consciousness.* Urbana: University of Illinois Press.

Kozinn, Allan. 2002. "Tin Cans, Silence, and a Cello." *NYT* (April 27).

Ledeen, Michael A. 2000. *Tocqueville on American Character: Why Tocqueville's Brilliant Exploration of the American Spirit Is as Vital and Important Today as It Was Nearly Two Hundred Years Ago.* New York: Truman Talley Books, St. Martin's Press.

List, George, and Juan Orrego-Salas, eds. 1967. *Music in the Americas.* The Hague: Mouton.

Marzorati, Gerald. 1999. "Sounds." *NYT Magazine* (December 5), 180.

Moore, Paul. n.d. Liner notes to *Portraits of Freedom*, Delos International DE3148.

Mostel, Raphael. 2002. "Freedom Is One Thing, but Liberty Is Going Too Far." *NYT* (April 9), 31, 37.

Nakai, R. Carlos, and AmoChip Dabney. 2001. Liner notes for *Edge of the Century*, Canyon Records CR-7034.

O'Brien, Geoffrey. 1998. "Recapturing the American Sound." *NYRB* (August 9), 45–51.

———. 1999. "Rock of Ages." *New York Review of Books* (December 16), 40–46.

Pareles, Jon. 1993. "It's Noisy! It's New! It's 90's." *NYT* (January 3), AR1.

———. 1999. "Working Hard so the Fans Can Party." *NYT* (October 30), AR1.

Partch, Harry. 1991. *Bitter Music: Collected Journals, Essays, Introductions, and Librettos*. Edited by Thomas McGeary. Urbana: University of Illinois Press.

Patterson, Orlando. 2000. "America's Worst Idea." *NYT Book Review* (October 22), 15–16.

Powers, Ann. 1999. "In Rock's Canon, Anyone and Everyone." *NYT* (December 26), AR1, 45.

Richardson, Lynda. 2000. "Jazz's Far-Reaching Riffs Resonate at Columbia." *NYT* (February 13), 39.

Ritter, F. L.1883. *Music in America.* New York: Scribner.

Rosen, Jody. 2000. "Two American Anthems in Two American Voices." *NYT* (July 2), 1, 28

Rothstein, Edward. 2000a. "Defending Lincoln's Legacy from a Confederacy of Culture Warriors." *NYT* (October 28), B13.

———. 2000b. "Seeking a Home in the Brave New World." *NYT* (January 1), 21.

Sachs, Joel. 1986. Liner notes to *Charles Ives the Visionary*, Musical Heritage Society MHS 512292Y.

Sandow, George. 2001. "Bring in the Noise." *NYT Book Review* (February 18).

Scherman, Tony. 1999. "Warhol: The Herald of Sampling." *NYT Book Review* (November 7), 46–49.

Shapiro, Michael. 1991. *The Sense of Change.* Bloomington: Indiana University Press.

Tocqueville, Alexis de. 1956 [1835, 1840]. *Democracy in America.* Edited by Richard D. Heffner. New York: New American Library/Penguin Putnam.

Todd, Richard. 2001. "Fragmented We Stand." *NYT Mazazine* (October 28), 15–16.

Tomassini, Anthony. 1999. "Composers for the Common Man: Aaron Copland, Champion of the American Sound." *NYT* (November 21), AR1, AR36.

———. 2000. "Music, Minus Those Pesky Composers." *NYT* (August 6), 28.

Udovitch, Mim. 2000. "It's All in the Mix." *NYT Book Review* (September 3), 11.

Weisbard, Eric. 2000. "Pop in the 90's: Everything for Everyone." *NYT* (April 30), 1, 18.

Whitman, Walt. 1855. *Leaves of Grass*. 1st ed., with an introduction by Malcolm Cowley. New York: Penguin Books.

Yates, Peter. 1967. *Twentieth-Century Music*. New York: Pantheon Books.

Resources

Videos

Jazz by Ken Burns. Video (10 videocassettes), DVD (10 discs), book, and CD (5 discs). PBS. An account of how jazz evolved from the blues, ragtime, swing, bebop, fusion. Features interviews, still photographs, archival film clips, and some 500 pieces of musical samples, complemented by and complementing the presentation of important jazz personalities.

American Roots Music. Video (4 videocassettes), DVD (2 discs), book, CD (4 discs). PBS. Features genres of what is often called folk music: blues, bluegrass, western swing, Native American music, zydeco, Tejano, etc. Performances, interviews, archival footage tracing the development of American music.

The History of Rock 'n' Roll. Video (10 videocassettes). PBS. Music performances from Elvis Presley to the Beatles to Public Enemy with commentaries from practitioners of the genre. Hundreds of songs.

The Big Band Sound of WWII. Videocassette, CD. Swing era hits including the "golden oldies," "Sentimental Journey," and "In the Mood" and dances.

Strange Fruit: The Story of a Song on Video. Video. (Can be ordered from California Newsreel, P. O. Box 2284, South Burlington, VT 05407. By phone: 877-811-7495; e-mail: contact@newsreel.org). A documentary on the song, its origins, and the notoriety it achieved after it was introduced by jazz great Billie Holiday, despite the ban by radio stations. It chronicles the history and legacy of the famed anti-lynching song "Strange Fruit" first made famous in 1939 by Holiday. The story is told against the background of race relations and the fight for civil rights. Includes the voices of Pete Seeger and veteran Civil Rights activist Rev. Dr. C. T. Vivan.

Standing in the Shadows of Motown, a documentary directed by Paul Justman, 2002. "An enlightening account of the Motown house band, the Funk Brothers"—Luc Sante in "One Nation Under a Groove", a review of Arthur Kempton's *Boogaloo: The Quintessence of American Popular Music* (Pantheon, 2003?)

Websites

Folkstreams.net. Films and videos about American traditional or "roots" culture.

Index